Times Tables Tests up to 12×12

Multiplication tables check

Samantha Townsend

William Collins' dream of knowledge for all began with the publication of his first book in 1819.
A self-educated mill worker, he not only enriched millions of lives, but also founded a flourishing
publishing house. Today, staying true to this spirit, Collins books are packed with inspiration,
innovation and practical expertise. They place you at the centre of a world of possibility
and give you exactly what you need to explore it.

Collins. Freedom to teach.

Collins
An imprint of HarperCollins*Publishers*
The News Building
1 London Bridge Street
London
SE1 9GF

Browse the complete Collins catalogue at **www.collins.co.uk**

© HarperCollins*Publishers* Limited 2018

10 9 8 7 6 5 4 3 2 1

ISBN 978-0-00-831156-8

British Library Cataloguing in Publication Data. A catalogue record for this publication is available from the British Library.

Author: Samantha Townsend
Publisher: Katie Sergeant
Senior Editor: Mike Appleton
Editorial packager: Life Lines Editorial Services
Reviewer: Peter Clarke
Cover designer: The Big Mountain Design, Ken Vail Graphic Design
Production controller: Katharine Willard
Printed and bound by CPI Group (UK) Ltd, Croydon, CR0 4YY

Contents

Year 4

Introduction

Collins Assessment Times Tables Tests includes 100 tests for your children in Years 2, 3 and 4 to build fluency, recall and understanding. They can be used to ensure weekly progression and coverage of the multiplication tables up to and including 12x12 specified by year in the National Curriculum 2014.

Multiplication tables check

From June 2020, all pupils at the end of Year 4 in England will take an online multiplication tables check (MTC) in June. The check will comprise 25 questions in 4–5 minutes. It aims to support pupils to master multiplication skills and will help to identify pupils who have not yet mastered this mathematical concept, so additional support can be provided.

The Standard and Testing Agency conducted user research and several trials in schools during 2018. They will use the results of the trials to develop the format of the test, the timing and accessibility and will publish an assessment framework during the 2018 to 2019 academic year. A national voluntary pilot will take place in June 2019 to allow schools to become familiar with the check before it becomes statutory in June 2020. Schools will have a 3-week window to administer the new test and teachers will have the flexibility to administer the check to individual pupils, small groups or the whole class at the same time.

How to use this book

There are 30 tests per year group, testing the multiplication tables specified in Years 2, 3 and 4 in the Mathematics programmes of study: key stages 1 and 2. Each set of 30 tests starts with the new multiplication tables introduced that year and then revisits the previous years' times tables. The additional 10 tests at the end of Year 4 cover all times tables up to and including 12x12 and are to help prepare pupils for the MTC.

Each test has a suggested timing, which is based on the number of questions in each test and the timings used in the MTC trials. The tests use a variety of formats to focus on procedural fluency. They also test for understanding and application of knowledge. Some variation questions are included to challenge more able pupils who may be working above expectations.

Answers

Answers are provided at the back of the book for quick marking.

Recording progress

You can use the pupil-facing record sheets to provide evidence of which areas the children have performed well in and where they need to focus. A spreadsheet is provided in the downloadable version so you can easily record results for your classes and analyse gaps to inform your next teaching and learning steps.

Editable download

All the files are available in Word and PDF format for you to edit if you wish. Go to Collins.co.uk/assessment/downloads to find the instructions on how to download. The files are password protected and the password clue are included on our website. You will need to use the clue to locate the password in your book.

Year 2

2 Times Tables

5 Times Tables

10 Times Tables

Mixed 2, 5 and 10 Times Tables

Name	Class	Date

Test 1

1. 2 × 1 =

2. 8 × 2 =

3. 2 × 7 =

4. 2 × 2 =

5. 2 × 4 =

6. 6 × 2 =

7. 2 × 3 =

8. 9 × 2 =

9. 2 × 5 =

10. 10 × 2 =

Total _____ / 10 marks

Year 2

Name	Class	Date

Test 2

 2 minutes

1. 3 × 2 = ☐

2. 2 × 11 = ☐

3. 5 × 2 = ☐

4. 2 × 6 = ☐

5. 9 × 2 = ☐

6. 2 × 12 = ☐

7. 10 × 2 = ☐

8. 2 × 4 = ☐

9. 7 × 2 = ☐

10. 2 × 8 = ☐

Total _____ / 10 marks

Name	Class	Date

Test 3

 2 minutes

1. $2 \times \boxed{} = 2$

2. $\boxed{} \times 2 = 4$

3. $2 \times \boxed{} = 18$

4. $\boxed{} \times 2 = 10$

5. $2 \times \boxed{} = 8$

6. $\boxed{} \times 2 = 12$

7. $2 \times \boxed{} = 16$

8. $\boxed{} \times 2 = 6$

9. $2 \times \boxed{} = 14$

10. $\boxed{} \times 2 = 22$

Total _____ / 10 marks

Name	Class	Date

Test 4

1. $4 \div 2 =$ □

2. $18 \div 2 =$ □

3. $20 \div 2 =$ □

4. $6 \div 2 =$ □

5. $12 \div 2 =$ □

6. $10 \div 2 =$ □

7. $14 \div 2 =$ □

8. $16 \div 2 =$ □

9. $8 \div 2 =$ □

10. $22 \div 2 =$ □

Total _____ / 10 marks

Year 2

Test 5

🕐 3 minutes

1. What is three multiplied by two? ☐

2. How many twos make ten? ☐

3. What are five lots of two? ☐

4. How many groups of two make fourteen? ☐

5. What is double eleven? ☐

6. What is nine added to itself? ☐

7. What is ten multiplied by two? ☐

8. What is six divided by two? ☐

9. What is two shared between two? ☐

10. What is half of twelve? ☐

Total _____ / 10 marks

Name	Class	Date

Test 6

1. There are 10 oranges ready for juicing. If each orange is cut in half, how many pieces of orange are there altogether? ☐

2. A tree grows 2 new buds every day. How many new buds does it grow in 7 days? ☐

3. Arjun has 3 friends over to play. If each friend eats 2 biscuits, how many biscuits do his friends eat in total? ☐

4. It takes Amaya 8 minutes to walk to school each day. How many minutes does it take her over 2 days? ☐ minutes

5. Rory buys 2 sweets that each cost 12p. How much do they cost altogether? ☐ p

Year 2

6. Mrs Potter hangs 11 pairs of socks on the washing line. What is the total number of socks she hangs on the washing line? ☐

7. If there are 6 cars travelling and 2 people in each car, how many people are travelling in cars? ☐

8. Melissa eats double the amount of sweets than her brother, Joe. If Joe eats 5 sweets, how many sweets does Melissa eat? ☐

9. If it takes 2 minutes to make a pancake, how long will it take to make 9 pancakes? ☐ minutes

10. If a plant grows 2 cm each week, how many centimetres will it grow in 4 weeks? ☐ cm

Total _____ / 10 marks

Test 7

1. There are 11 pairs of gloves in lost property. How many gloves are there in total? ☐

2. $18 \div 2 =$ ☐

3. ☐ $\times 2 = 14$

4. What is double 10? ☐

5. How many legs do 3 birds have? ☐

6. $12 \div$ ☐ $= 6$

7. How many twos make eight? ☐

8. Luke has 6 stickers from his comics. If he collects 2 stickers a week, how many weeks has he been collecting stickers? ☐

9. ☐ $\div 5 = 2$

10. ☐ $\times 2 = 4$

Total _____ / 10 marks

Name	Class	Date

Test 8

 2 minutes

1. 8 × 5 =

2. 5 × 7 =

3. 11 × 5 =

4. 5 × 3 =

5. 9 × 5 =

6. 5 × 5 =

7. 5 × 4 =

8. 10 × 5 =

9. 5 × 6 =

10. 12 × 5 =

Total _____ / 10 marks

 Year 2

Name	Class	Date

Test 9

 2 minutes

1. $3 \times 5 =$ ☐

2. $5 \times 9 =$ ☐

3. $5 \times 12 =$ ☐

4. $6 \times 5 =$ ☐

5. $5 \times 11 =$ ☐

6. $4 \times 5 =$ ☐

7. $8 \times 5 =$ ☐

8. $2 \times 5 =$ ☐

9. $7 \times 5 =$ ☐

10. $5 \times 5 =$ ☐

Total _____ / 10 marks

   Year 2

Name	Class	Date

Test 10

1. ☐ × 5 = 10

2. 5 × ☐ = 20

3. ☐ × 5 = 45

4. 5 × ☐ = 55

5. ☐ × 5 = 15

6. 5 × ☐ = 60

7. ☐ × 5 = 50

8. 5 × ☐ = 30

9. ☐ × 5 = 25

10. 5 × ☐ = 35

Total _____ / 10 marks

Test 11

 2 minutes

1. 55 ÷ 5 = ☐

2. 35 ÷ 5 = ☐

3. 15 ÷ 5 = ☐

4. 45 ÷ 5 = ☐

5. 10 ÷ 5 = ☐

6. 40 ÷ 5 = ☐

7. 5 ÷ 5 = ☐

8. 50 ÷ 5 = ☐

9. 30 ÷ 5 = ☐

10. 25 ÷ 5 = ☐

Total _____ / 10 marks

Test 12

1. What do five groups of five equal? ☐

2. What is five multiplied by ten? ☐

3. How many groups of five make fifteen? ☐

4. What is forty divided by five? ☐

5. What is four multiplied by five? ☐

6. What is five multiplied by seven? ☐

7. How many fives are in forty-five? ☐

8. What is thirty divided by five? ☐

9. How many groups of five are in sixty? ☐

10. What do eleven groups of five equal? ☐

Total _____ / 10 marks

Name	Class	Date

Test 13

1. Lucia has 5 coins. If she shares them equally between her 5 friends, how many coins do they each get? ☐

2. Jack has saved £45 pocket money. If he gets £5 every week, how many weeks has he been saving? ☐

3. Pentagons have 5 sides. How many sides are there on 3 pentagons? ☐

4. Pears come in packs of 5. How many pears are in 10 packs? ☐

5. There are 5 classes in a school. Each class has 12 fish in their tank. How many fish are there in the school? ☐

6. There are 30 people in a café. If each table is filled with 5 people, how many tables are there? ☐

7. Imran shares 35 sweets between 5 friends. How many sweets do they each get? ☐

8. Rosie has a pack of 20 colouring pencils. If there are 5 different colours in the pack, how many of each colour pencil does she have, if there is the same number of each colour? ☐

9. If pies are cut into 5 slices, how many slices would there be in 2 pies? ☐

10. At the zoo there are 11 penguins in an enclosure. If each penguin eats 5 fish a day, how many fish does the zookeeper need? ☐

Total _____ / 10 marks

Name	Class	Date

Test 14

 3 minutes

1. $40 \div 5 = \boxed{}$

2. $\boxed{} \times 5 = 30$

3. Frogs have 4 feet. How many feet are there on 5 frogs? $\boxed{}$

4. $\boxed{} \div 5 = 7$

5. What is five multiplied by itself? $\boxed{}$

6. How many fives make fifteen? $\boxed{}$

7. $20 \div \boxed{} = 5$

8. $9 \times 5 = \boxed{}$

9. There are 50 children in a year group at school. How many groups of 5 can the children make? $\boxed{}$

10. $\boxed{} \times 5 = 60$

Total _____ / 10 marks

Test 15

 2 minutes

1. 1 × 10 =

2. 8 × 10 =

3. 10 × 2 =

4. 10 × 10 =

5. 7 × 10 =

6. 10 × 5 =

7. 10 × 3 =

8. 11 × 10 =

9. 6 × 10 =

10. 10 × 9 =

Total _____ / 10 marks

Year 2

Name	Class	Date

Test 16

 2 minutes

1. 9 × 10 =

2. 10 × 1 =

3. 2 × 10 =

4. 5 × 10 =

5. 11 × 10 =

6. 10 × 12 =

7. 10 × 10 =

8. 3 × 10 =

9. 10 × 4 =

10. 10 × 6 =

Total _____ / 10 marks

                   Year 2

Name	Class	Date

Test 17

1. ☐ × 10 = 80

2. 10 × ☐ = 120

3. ☐ × 10 = 20

4. 10 × ☐ = 60

5. ☐ × 10 = 40

6. 10 × ☐ = 100

7. ☐ × 10 = 30

8. 10 × ☐ = 70

9. ☐ × 10 = 50

10. 10 × ☐ = 90

Total _____ / 10 marks

Test 18

1. 20 ÷ 10 =

2. 40 ÷ 10 =

3. 60 ÷ 10 =

4. 90 ÷ 10 =

5. 110 ÷ 10 =

6. 50 ÷ 10 =

7. 100 ÷ 10 =

8. 30 ÷ 10 =

9. 120 ÷ 10 =

10. 70 ÷ 10 =

Total _____ / 10 marks

Name	Class	Date

Test 19

 3 minutes

1. What is four multiplied by ten? ☐

2. How many tens go into fifty? ☐

3. What is ten multiplied by nine? ☐

4. What is seventy shared between ten? ☐

5. How many groups of ten are there in thirty? ☐

6. What is ten multiplied by itself? ☐

7. How many times does ten go into ten? ☐

8. What is one hundred and twenty shared between ten? ☐

9. What are two lots of ten? ☐

10. What do eleven groups of ten equal? ☐

Total _____ / 10 marks

Year 2

Test 20

1. Carpet comes in 10 m rolls. How many metres of carpet would there be in 8 rolls? ☐ m

2. There are 70 pieces of chocolate in a giant bar. If there are 10 rows of chocolate in the bar, how many pieces are in each row? ☐

3. A gardener plants 10 bulbs in each flowerpot. How many bulbs are needed in 12 pots? ☐

4. Safia spends 50p on lollies. If each lolly costs 10p, how many lollies does she buy? ☐

5. Rory reads 10 pages of his book every day for 6 days. How many pages does he read in total? ☐

6. There are 90 children in a school show. If they are divided into 10 equal dancing groups, how many children are in each group? ☐

7. There are 10 teams in a cycling race. If there are 2 people in each team, how many people are in the race? ☐

8. A group of children are counting their toes. In total they have 30 toes. How many children are there? ☐

9. Potatoes come in 10 kg bags. What would the weight of 10 bags be? ☐ kg

10. Stefan counts 40 pens. If there are 10 pens in a pack, how many packs does he have? ☐

Total _____ **/ 10 marks**

Name	Class	Date

Test 21

1. There are ten years in a decade. How many decades has a 40-year-old person been alive? ☐

2. ☐ × 10 = 20

3. 100 ÷ ☐ = 10

4. How many groups of ten make ninety? ☐

5. Crisps come in multipacks of 10. How many packets of crisps are there in 7 multipacks? ☐

6. How many tens make eighty? ☐

7. 12 × 10 = ☐

8. Ahmed saves £10 a week. How much money does he save in 11 weeks? £ ☐

9. 10 × ☐ = 30

10. ☐ ÷ 10 = 5

Total _____ / 10 marks

 Year 2

Name	Class	Date

Test 22

 3 minutes

1. 2 × 10 = ☐

2. 5 × 7 = ☐

3. 4 × 5 = ☐

4. 10 × 6 = ☐

5. 2 × 2 = ☐

6. 5 × 10 = ☐

7. 6 × 2 = ☐

8. 9 × 5 = ☐

9. 3 × 2 = ☐

10. 10 × 10 = ☐

11. 8 × 10 = ☐

12. 2 × 11 = ☐

13. 3 × 5 = ☐

14. 11 × 5 = ☐

15. 12 × 2 = ☐

Total _____ / 15 marks

| Name | Class | Date |

Test 23

 3 minutes

1. $5 \times 2 =$ ☐

2. $4 \times 10 =$ ☐

3. $8 \times 5 =$ ☐

4. $2 \times 4 =$ ☐

5. $7 \times 10 =$ ☐

6. $12 \times 5 =$ ☐

7. $2 \times 9 =$ ☐

8. $8 \times 2 =$ ☐

9. $12 \times 10 =$ ☐

10. $10 \times 9 =$ ☐

11. $7 \times 2 =$ ☐

12. $6 \times 5 =$ ☐

13. $10 \times 11 =$ ☐

14. $3 \times 10 =$ ☐

15. $5 \times 5 =$ ☐

Total _____ / 15 marks

Year 2

Test 24

 3 minutes

1. $25 \div 5 =$ ☐

2. $14 \div 2 =$ ☐

3. $30 \div 10 =$ ☐

4. $4 \div 2 =$ ☐

5. $70 \div 10 =$ ☐

6. $50 \div 5 =$ ☐

7. $16 \div 2 =$ ☐

8. $60 \div 5 =$ ☐

9. $10 \div 2 =$ ☐

10. $100 \div 10 =$ ☐

11. $20 \div 5 =$ ☐

12. $35 \div 5 =$ ☐

13. $80 \div 10 =$ ☐

14. $24 \div 2 =$ ☐

15. $120 \div 10 =$ ☐

Total _____ / 15 marks

Year 2

Name	Class	Date

Test 25

 3 minutes

1. $2 \div 2 =$ ☐

2. $20 \div 2 =$ ☐

3. $25 \div 5 =$ ☐

4. $40 \div 5 =$ ☐

5. $90 \div 10 =$ ☐

6. $12 \div 2 =$ ☐

7. $55 \div 5 =$ ☐

8. $15 \div 5 =$ ☐

9. $10 \div 10 =$ ☐

10. $60 \div 10 =$ ☐

11. $24 \div 2 =$ ☐

12. $40 \div 10 =$ ☐

13. $10 \div 5 =$ ☐

14. $45 \div 5 =$ ☐

15. $30 \div 5 =$ ☐

Total _____ / 15 marks

Test 26

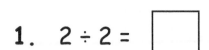 3 minutes

1. 2 ÷ 2 = ☐

2. 4 × ☐ = 40

3. ☐ ÷ 2 = 5

4. 10 × ☐ = 80

5. 60 ÷ 5 = ☐

6. ☐ × 5 = 30

7. 20 ÷ ☐ = 2

8. 10 × 2 = ☐

9. 110 ÷ 10 = ☐

10. 2 × 11 = ☐

11. 90 ÷ ☐ = 10

12. 5 × ☐ = 45

13. 30 ÷ 10 = ☐

14. ☐ × 2 = 22

15. 15 ÷ 5 = ☐

Total _____ / 15 marks

Year 2

Test 27

🕐 4 minutes

1. What is two multiplied by five? ☐

2. How many times does five go into twenty? ☐

3. What is ten multiplied by itself? ☐

4. What do ten groups of eight equal? ☐

5. How many tens are there in sixty? ☐

6. What is thirty-five shared between five? ☐

7. What are ten groups of seven? ☐

8. How many fives go into forty? ☐

9. What do nine groups of two equal? ☐

10. How many twos go into sixteen? ☐

11. How many times does ten go into one hundred? ☐

12. What do five lots of six equal? ☐

13. How many twos are there in twenty? ☐

14. What is five multiplied by nine? ☐

15. How many lots of ten in eighty? ☐

Total _____ / 15 marks

Name	Class	Date

Test 28

 4 minutes

1. If there are 5 eggs in 1 basket, how many eggs are there in 3 baskets?

2. On a pond there are 12 ducklings. If each mother duck

   has two ducklings, how many mother ducks are on the

   pond?

3. A class of 30 children go camping. If there are 10 tents, how many

   children will there be in each tent?

4. Otis spends his £10 pocket money on ice creams. Each ice cream costs

   £2. How many ice creams does he buy?

5. If it costs £50 for 10 children to go on a trip, how much does it cost

   for each child? £

6. There are 7 sets of swings at a park. If there are 2 swings in each set,

   how many swings are in the park?

7. James walks his dog for 10 minutes every morning. How many minutes

   does he walk his dog in 7 days? minutes

8. Mum makes 35 biscuits for her 5 children. How many biscuits can they each have? ▢

9. There are 4 light switches in each room of a house. If there are 10 rooms in the house, how many light switches are there? ▢

10. Arthur gives out 25 balloons to 5 friends at the end of his party. How many balloons does each friend get to take home? ▢

11. If 8 trains come through a station every hour, how many trains will pass through the station in 5 hours? ▢

12. Beetles have six legs. How many legs do 5 beetles have? ▢

13. If a bird catches 2 worms every minute, how many worms can it catch in 4 minutes? ▢

14. There are 5 butterflies in the garden and each one has 4 spots. How many spots are on the butterflies altogether? ▢

15. An aeroplane can take 60 passengers. If 5 people can sit in each row, how many rows of seats are there on the aeroplane? ▢

Total _____ / 15 marks

Name	Class	Date

Test 29

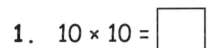 3 minutes

1. 10 × 10 = ☐

2. 2 × 20 = ☐

3. 6 × 50 = ☐

4. 40 × 2 = ☐

5. 8 × 20 = ☐

6. 12 × 5 = ☐

7. 7 × 10 = ☐

8. 20 × 6 = ☐

9. 50 × 1 = ☐

10. 12 × 10 = ☐

11. 30 × 2 = ☐

12. 40 × 1 = ☐

13. 100 × 2 = ☐

14. 5 × 20 = ☐

15. 20 × 7 = ☐

Total _____ / 15 marks

Year 2

Test 30

 4 minutes

1. $11 \times 5 =$ ☐

2. $100 \div$ ☐ $= 10$

3. $8 \times 10 =$ ☐

4. What do ten groups of five equal? ☐

5. Dinah rolls two dice, and they both land on a 5. What is the total number she has rolled on both dice? ☐

6. ☐ $\div 2 = 7$

7. How many groups of ten make sixty? ☐

8. What is five multiplied by itself? ☐

9. What do two lots of ten equal? ☐

10. ☐ $\div 5 = 12$

11. How many groups of ten make 120? ☐

12. If Archie practises the piano for 2 hours every day, how many hours will he practise in 8 days? ☐ hours

13. $40 \div \boxed{} = 10$

14. $24 \div 2 = \boxed{}$

15. Laura makes packs of beads for her 10 classmates. If she puts 11 beads in each pack, how many beads will she need altogether? ☐

Total _____ **/ 15 marks**

Year 3

3 Times Tables

4 Times Tables

8 Times Tables

Mixed 3, 4 and 8 Times Tables

Mixed 2, 3, 4, 5, 8 and 10 Times Tables

Name	Class	Date

Test 1

 2 minutes

1. 2 × 3 = ☐

2. 3 × 6 = ☐

3. 12 × 3 = ☐

4. 3 × 3 = ☐

5. 8 × 3 = ☐

6. 3 × 4 = ☐

7. 7 × 3 = ☐

8. 3 × 5 = ☐

9. 10 × 3 = ☐

10. 3 × 9 = ☐

11. 1 × 3 = ☐

12. 3 × 11 = ☐

Total _____ / 12 marks

Name	Class	Date

Test 2

1. ▢ × 3 = 6

2. 15 ÷ ▢ = 5

3. 8 × 3 = ▢

4. ▢ ÷ 3 = 4

5. 10 × ▢ = 30

6. 9 ÷ 3 = ▢

7. ▢ × 3 = 36

8. 18 ÷ ▢ = 3

9. 9 × 3 = ▢

10. ▢ ÷ 3 = 7

11. 3 × ▢ = 33

12. 3 ÷ 3 = ▢

Total _____ / 12 marks

Year 3

Test 3

🕐 3 minutes

1. If a triangle has 3 sides, how many sides are there on 12 triangles?

2. Sanjay picks flowers for his 3 daughters. If he picks 30 flowers altogether, how many flowers will each daughter get?

3. If Maya shares 9 plums between her 3 friends, how many plums will each friend get?

4. There are 4 children playing on tricycles. If a tricycle has 3 wheels, how many wheels will there be altogether?

5. If a teacher orders a box of 36 pairs of scissors and there are 3 classes in the school, how many pairs of scissors will each class get?

6. There are 33 pupils in a class. How many groups of 3 can the pupils make?

Year 3

7. Balls of string come in 3 m lengths. How many metres of string are there in 9 balls? ☐ m

8. If 8 children are playing marbles and they each bring 3 marbles to the game, how many marbles will there be in total? ☐

9. If 3 eggs are needed to make a cake, how many eggs will be needed for 5 cakes? ☐

10. Natalie buys a pack of 3 T-shirts. If the pack costs £21, how much does each T-shirt cost? £ ☐

11. Kimiko walks her dog 3 times a day. How many walks does she go on in 10 days? ☐

12. If Dad makes 3 cups of tea and adds two teaspoons of sugar to each cup, how many teaspoons of sugar does he use? ☐

Total _____ / 12 marks

Test 4

 2 minutes

1. 100 × 3 = ☐

2. 2 × 30 = ☐

3. 60 × 3 = ☐

4. 90 × 3 = ☐

5. 3 × 20 = ☐

6. 30 × 7 = ☐

7. 12 × 3 = ☐

8. 3 × 80 = ☐

9. 40 × 3 = ☐

10. 11 × 30 = ☐

11. 5 × 30 = ☐

12. 30 × 3 = ☐

Total _____ / 12 marks

Name	Class	Date

Test 5

 3 minutes

1. What do five groups of three equal? ☐

2. 11 × 3 = ☐

3. 21 ÷ ☐ = 3

4. Aisha has 36p. If she buys some sweets that cost 3p each, how many sweets can she buy? ☐

5. 8 × 3 = ☐

6. What is one-third of 36? ☐

7. Ingrid has collected 18 stamps. If she collected the same number of stamps from 3 different countries, how many stamps did she get from each country? ☐

8. What is three multiplied by itself? ☐

9. What is twenty-seven shared between three? ☐

10. $30 \div 3 = \boxed{}$

11. $24 \div 3 = \boxed{}$

12. Abdu makes 2 drinks. If he pours 30 ml of orange squash into each cup, how many millilitres of orange squash does he use? $\boxed{}$ ml

Total _____ / 12 marks

Name	Class	Date

Test 6

 2 minutes

1. 4 × 1 =

2. 7 × 4 =

3. 2 × 4 =

4. 10 × 4 =

5. 4 × 5 =

6. 12 × 4 =

7. 4 × 11 =

8. 4 × 4 =

9. 6 × 4 =

10. 4 × 8 =

11. 3 × 4 =

12. 9 × 4 =

Total _____ / 12 marks

Test 7

 2 minutes

1. $4 \div 4 =$ ☐

2. ☐ $\times 4 = 44$

3. $12 \div$ ☐ $= 3$

4. $36 \div 4 =$ ☐

5. ☐ $\times 5 = 20$

6. $28 \div$ ☐ $= 7$

7. $12 \times 4 =$ ☐

8. $8 \div 4 =$ ☐

9. $4 \times$ ☐ $= 16$

10. $6 \times 4 =$ ☐

11. $40 \div 4 =$ ☐

12. $4 \times$ ☐ $= 32$ Total _____ / 12 marks

Test 8

1. A family of 4 go on holiday. If they each take 5 pairs of shorts, how many pairs of shorts do they pack? ☐

2. It costs £4 to get into the local zoo. How much will it cost for 11 children to go to the zoo? £ ☐

3. If Jonah has 4 bananas and gives one to each of his 4 friends, how many bananas do they each get? ☐

4. If a house has 8 windows, how many windows do 4 houses have? ☐

5. Dad feeds the cats 8 pouches of cat food during the day. If there are 4 cats, how many pouches does each cat get? ☐

6. If Hiromi earns £12 for babysitting for 4 hours, how much does she earn an hour? £ ☐

7. Emilio picks 24 apples from his tree. If he sells them in bags of 4, how many bags of apples will he have? ☐

8. A farmer has 48 kg of carrots in his store. If he puts the carrots into 4 equal sacks, how many kilograms will each sack weigh? ☐ kg

9. Cupcakes come in boxes of 9. How many cakes are there in 4 boxes? ☐

10. Alfie is working with some shapes. If each shape has 4 sides and he counts 16 sides, how many shapes does he have? ☐

11. In a train carriage there are 4 seats in each row. How many seats are there in 7 rows? ☐

12. Matthew has saved £40. If he gets £4 pocket money a week, how many weeks has it taken him to save the money? ☐

Total _____ / 12 marks

Name	Class	Date

Test 9

 2 minutes

1. 100 × 4 =

2. 4 × 11 =

3. 40 × 5 =

4. 12 × 4 =

5. 70 × 4 =

6. 4 × 40 =

7. 80 × 4 =

8. 40 × 9 =

9. 40 × 3 =

10. 6 × 40 =

11. 10 × 40 =

12. 20 × 4 =

Total _____ / 12 marks

Name	Class	Date

Test 10

 3 minutes

1. $2 \times 4 = \boxed{}$

2. $28 \div 4 = \boxed{}$

3. $4 \times \boxed{} = 40$

4. What is sixteen shared between four? $\boxed{}$

5. Zac takes his three friends to the cinema. It costs £4 for each ticket. How much money does he pay in total for himself and his friends? £ $\boxed{}$

6. $12 \times 4 = \boxed{}$

7. $4 \div \boxed{} = 1$

8. $\boxed{} \times 4 = 44$

9. What is thirty-six divided by four? $\boxed{}$

10. If five cats have four kittens each, how many kittens do they have altogether? ☐

11. 12 ÷ 4 = ☐

12. 24 ÷ 4 = ☐

Total _____ **/ 12 marks**

Test 11

 2 minutes

1. 2 × 8 =

2. 8 × 1 =

3. 9 × 8 =

4. 10 × 8 =

5. 12 × 8 =

6. 8 × 3 =

7. 5 × 8 =

8. 8 × 4 =

9. 6 × 8 =

10. 11 × 8 =

11. 7 × 8 =

12. 8 × 8 =

Total _____ / 12 marks

Name	Class	Date

Test 12

1. $8 \times 7 = \boxed{}$

2. $\boxed{} \times 8 = 80$

3. $24 \div \boxed{} = 8$

4. $32 \div 8 = \boxed{}$

5. $\boxed{} \times 8 = 24$

6. $8 \div \boxed{} = 1$

7. $6 \times 8 = \boxed{}$

8. $\boxed{} \times 8 = 40$

9. $16 \div \boxed{} = 8$

10. $9 \times 8 = \boxed{}$

11. $\boxed{} \times 8 = 96$

12. $88 \div \boxed{} = 8$

Total _____ / 12 marks

Year 3

Test 13

🕐 3 minutes

1. If one spider has 8 legs, how many legs are there on 5 spiders? ☐

2. Jafari is 6 years old; his father is 8 times older. How old is his father? ☐

3. A carpet fitter has 72 m of carpet and he needs to cut this into 8 m lengths. How many lengths will he cut? ☐

4. A fire engine has 2 ladders, which each extend to 8 m. What is the total length of both ladders? ☐ m

5. Eliana swims 8 widths of a pool. If the pool is 12 m wide, how far did she swim? ☐ m

6. A group of children raised a total of £80 for charity. If they each raised £8, how many children were raising money? ☐

7. If a roller skater travels 8 kilometres every hour, how far does she travel in 8 hours? ☐ km

8. There are 40 people seated on a boat. If they are sitting in rows of 8, how many rows of seats will the people take up? ☐

9. A teacher orders some new whiteboards; they come in packs of 8. If he orders 7 packs, how many whiteboards will be delivered to the school? ☐

10. What is £32 shared between 8 people? £ ☐

11. Granny makes a tray of 24 brownies and shares them with her 8 grandchildren. How many brownies does each grandchild get? ☐

12. Eleven children go to a party, and each eat eight sweets. How many sweets do they eat altogether? ☐

Total _____ / 12 marks

Name	Class	Date

Test 14

 2 minutes

1. 10 × 8 =

2. 3 × 80 =

3. 50 × 8 =

4. 9 × 80 =

5. 8 × 100 =

6. 11 × 8 =

7. 60 × 8 =

8. 80 × 7 =

9. 12 × 8 =

10. 80 × 8 =

11. 2 × 80 =

12. 40 × 8 =

Total _____ / 12 marks

Test 15

 3 minutes

1. $6 \times 8 = \boxed{}$

2. $40 \div \boxed{} = 8$

3. What is eight multiplied by twelve? $\boxed{}$

4. $\boxed{} \div 8 = 8$

5. In a decathlon there are 10 events. If each event takes 8 minutes, how long will the decathlon take to complete? $\boxed{}$ minutes

6. How many times does eight go into forty-eight? $\boxed{}$

7. $56 \div 8 = \boxed{}$

8. A builder needs 24 tiles for a job. If tiles come in packs of 8, how many packs of tiles does he need to buy? $\boxed{}$

9. $\boxed{} \times 8 = 72$

10. If Benji saves £11 a week for 8 weeks, how much money does he save? £ ☐

11. What is two multiplied by eight? ☐

12. ☐ ÷ 8 = 1

Total _____ / 12 marks

| Name | Class | Date |

Test 16

 3-4 minutes

1. 1 × 3 = ☐

2. 3 × 6 = ☐

3. 8 × 3 = ☐

4. 10 × 8 = ☐

5. 2 × 4 = ☐

6. 10 × 3 = ☐

7. 8 × 12 = ☐

8. 7 × 4 = ☐

9. 6 × 8 = ☐

10. 4 × 11 = ☐

11. 4 × 3 = ☐

12. 8 × 2 = ☐

13. 7 × 8 = ☐

14. 5 × 4 = ☐

15. 3 × 3 = ☐

16. 8 × 4 = ☐

17. 12 × 3 = ☐

18. 4 × 1 = ☐

19. 8 × 8 = ☐

20. 9 × 4 = ☐

Total _____ / 20 marks

Test 17

🕐 3-4 minutes

1. 1 × 8 = ☐

2. 7 × 3 = ☐

3. 4 × 4 = ☐

4. 3 × 8 = ☐

5. 10 × 4 = ☐

6. 3 × 9 = ☐

7. 4 × 7 = ☐

8. 11 × 3 = ☐

9. 8 × 9 = ☐

10. 3 × 1 = ☐

11. 11 × 8 = ☐

12. 4 × 2 = ☐

13. 5 × 3 = ☐

14. 8 × 8 = ☐

15. 3 × 6 = ☐

16. 4 × 12 = ☐

17. 7 × 8 = ☐

18. 6 × 4 = ☐

19. 3 × 6 = ☐

20. 11 × 4 = ☐

Total _____ / 20 marks

Year 3

Test 18

🕐 3–4 minutes

1. $2 \times 3 = \boxed{}$

2. $\boxed{} \times 3 = 12$

3. $10 \times \boxed{} = 40$

4. $7 \times 4 = \boxed{}$

5. $\boxed{} \times 8 = 48$

6. $3 \times \boxed{} = 27$

7. $3 \times 8 = \boxed{}$

8. $\boxed{} \times 5 = 40$

9. $10 \times \boxed{} = 80$

10. $7 \times 8 = \boxed{}$

11. $\boxed{} \times 8 = 16$

12. $4 \times \boxed{} = 20$

13. $12 \times 8 = \boxed{}$

14. $\boxed{} \times 3 = 18$

15. $6 \times \boxed{} = 24$

16. $4 \times 9 = \boxed{}$

17. $\boxed{} \times 4 = 32$

18. $8 \times \boxed{} = 64$

19. $11 \times 4 = \boxed{}$

20. $\boxed{} \times 3 = 36$

Total _____ **/ 20 marks**

Test 19

🕐 3-4 minutes

1. $8 \div 4 =$

2. $9 \div 3 =$

3. $24 \div 8 =$

4. $72 \div 8 =$

5. $16 \div 4 =$

6. $88 \div 8 =$

7. $36 \div 3 =$

8. $56 \div 8 =$

9. $48 \div 8 =$

10. $32 \div 4 =$

11. $21 \div 3 =$

12. $24 \div 8 =$

13. $18 \div 3 =$

14. $36 \div 4 =$

15. $33 \div 3 =$

16. $16 \div 8 =$

17. $40 \div 4 =$

18. $40 \div 8 =$

19. $27 \div 3 =$

20. $20 \div 4 =$

Total _____ / 20 marks

Year 3

Name	Class	Date

Test 20

1. What does one group of three equal? ☐

2. How many groups of eight are there in eighty? ☐

3. What is three multiplied by itself? ☐

4. What is thirty shared between three? ☐

5. What is double four? ☐

6. How many groups of four make twenty-eight? ☐

7. What are four groups of three? ☐

8. How many times does four go into thirty-two? ☐

9. What do seven groups of eight equal? ☐

10. What are two groups of eight? ☐

11. What do three lots of twelve equal? ☐

12. What is twenty divided into four equal groups? ☐

13. How many fours go into twelve? □

14. What is four shared between four? □

15. What is eight multiplied by eight? □

16. How many groups of three make eighteen? □

17. What is twelve multiplied by eight? □

18. What is forty-four shared between four? □

19. What is nine multiplied by four? □

20. How many times does twelve go into ninety-six? □

Total _____ / 20 marks

Name	Class	Date

Test 21

1. If 3 garden gnomes each have 10 fish, how many fish do they have in total? ☐

2. Pim goes to gymnastics practice 3 days a week; she practises for 9 hours a week. How many hours does she practise each day? ☐ hours

3. In a game of ten pin bowls each pin is worth 8 points.

    If 9 pins are knocked down, how many points are scored? ☐

4. If 5 children each read 3 books, how many books do they read altogether? ☐

5. Anja bakes 21 cookies for herself and 2 friends. How many cookies does each person get? ☐

6. Jacob's hand span measures 9 cm. What would 3 of his hand spans measure? ☐ cm

7. If 3 friends share 33 marbles equally between themselves, how many marbles do they each get? ☐

8. If there are 8 people travelling in cars and there are 4 people in each car, how many cars are travelling? ☐

9. If a square has 4 equal sides and each side is 8 cm, what is the total length of its sides? ☐ cm

10. There are 24 rabbits in a pen; at night, they are put equally into 4 separate hutches. How many rabbits are in each hutch? ☐

11. Sixty-four spectators attend a school sports day; they are seated on benches for 8 people. How many benches are required? ☐

12. Three dogs are out for a walk with their owner. How many dogs' legs are there? ☐

13. A play is 40 minutes long. If it is split into 4 equal acts, how long is each act? ☐ minutes

14. Jake lines up 4 pencils. If each pencil measures 12 cm, what is the total length of the pencils? ☐ cm

15. If an octopus has 8 tentacles, how many tentacles would 3 octopuses have? ☐

16. On a ferry there are 88 people. If each lifeboat on the ferry holds 8 people, how many lifeboats would be needed in an emergency?

17. An octagon is an 8-sided shape. How many sides would there be on 7 octagons?

18. Elijah runs for 40 minutes. If it takes him 8 minutes to run a kilometre, how many kilometres does he run? km

19. A teacher gives 4 stickers to each of his top 4 pupils. How many stickers does he give out altogether?

20. It takes Rowan 12 minutes to walk to school. How many minutes will he spend walking to school over 3 days? minutes

Total _____ / 20 marks

Test 22

 5 minutes

1. $1 \times 8 =$ ☐

2. $24 \div$ ☐ $= 3$

3. If a man runs 3 km every morning with his dog, how many kilometres does he run in 7 days? ☐ km

4. What is four multiplied by itself? ☐

5. What is forty shared between four? ☐

6. A class of 27 pupils are asked to get into groups of 3. How many groups can they make? ☐

7. $4 \times$ ☐ $= 28$

8. How many times does three go into thirty-three? ☐

9. $9 \times 8 =$ ☐

10. What is three multiplied by one? ☐

11. $88 \div 8 =$ ☐

12. What is four multiplied by two? ☐

13. What do six groups of three equal? ☐

14. $15 \div 3 =$ ☐

15. The total length of a regular octagon's sides is 64 cm. If an octagon has 8 sides, how long is one side? ☐ cm

16. What is one-quarter of 32? ☐

17. If 8 children eat an ice cream every day for 7 days on holiday, how many ice creams do they eat altogether? ☐

18. At a ski resort it snows for 8 cm a day every day. How much snow will fall in 6 days? ☐ cm

19. $24 \div$ ☐ $= 4$

20. What is eleven multiplied by four? ☐

Total _____ / 20 marks

Name	Class	Date

Test 23

1. 8 × 2 = ☐

2. 4 × 9 = ☐

3. 10 × 6 = ☐

4. 8 × 5 = ☐

5. 12 × 10 = ☐

6. 5 × 6 = ☐

7. 2 × 7 = ☐

8. 9 × 4 = ☐

9. 11 × 3 = ☐

10. 12 × 2 = ☐

11. 8 × 10 = ☐

12. 6 × 2 = ☐

13. 4 × 5 = ☐

14. 11 × 8 = ☐

15. 12 × 4 = ☐

16. 8 × 7 = ☐

17. 3 × 8 = ☐

18. 5 × 8 = ☐

19. 7 × 3 = ☐

20. 3 × 2 = ☐

Total _____ / 20 marks

Name	Class	Date

Test 24

 3–4 minutes

1. 1 × 3 = ☐

2. 8 × 4 = ☐

3. 4 × 2 = ☐

4. 5 × 5 = ☐

5. 7 × 4 = ☐

6. 2 × 11 = ☐

7. 6 × 5 = ☐

8. 10 × 7 = ☐

9. 2 × 9 = ☐

10. 10 × 9 = ☐

11. 3 × 8 = ☐

12. 3 × 3 = ☐

13. 11 × 10 = ☐

14. 8 × 12 = ☐

15. 1 × 4 = ☐

16. 4 × 10 = ☐

17. 5 × 2 = ☐

18. 9 × 8 = ☐

19. 12 × 5 = ☐

20. 6 × 3 = ☐

Total _____ / 20 marks

Year 3

Test 25

🕐 3-4 minutes

1. $4 \div 2 =$ ☐

2. $50 \div 10 =$ ☐

3. $60 \div 10 =$ ☐

4. $32 \div 4 =$ ☐

5. $33 \div 3 =$ ☐

6. $88 \div 8 =$ ☐

7. $16 \div 4 =$ ☐

8. $15 \div 3 =$ ☐

9. $12 \div 2 =$ ☐

10. $30 \div 5 =$ ☐

11. $24 \div 4 =$ ☐

12. $20 \div 10 =$ ☐

13. $72 \div 8 =$ ☐

14. $16 \div 2 =$ ☐

15. $27 \div 3 =$ ☐

16. $40 \div 5 =$ ☐

17. $80 \div 8 =$ ☐

18. $56 \div 8 =$ ☐

19. $60 \div 5 =$ ☐

20. $36 \div 4 =$ ☐

Total _____ / 20 marks

Name	Class	Date

Test 26

 3–4 minutes

1. 6 ÷ 2 = ☐

2. 12 ÷ 3 = ☐

3. 35 ÷ 5 = ☐

4. 44 ÷ 4 = ☐

5. 36 ÷ 4 = ☐

6. 64 ÷ 8 = ☐

7. 120 ÷ 10 = ☐

8. 36 ÷ 3 = ☐

9. 70 ÷ 10 = ☐

10. 18 ÷ 3 = ☐

11. 80 ÷ 8 = ☐

12. 24 ÷ 8 = ☐

13. 14 ÷ 2 = ☐

14. 28 ÷ 4 = ☐

15. 48 ÷ 8 = ☐

16. 18 ÷ 2 = ☐

17. 55 ÷ 5 = ☐

18. 45 ÷ 5 = ☐

19. 96 ÷ 8 = ☐

20. 110 ÷ 10 = ☐

Total _____ / 20 marks

Test 27

1. $5 \times 2 =$

2. $100 \div 10 =$

3. $8 \times 7 =$

4. $25 \div 5 =$

5. $90 \div 10 =$

6. $10 \times 10 =$

7. $16 \div 8 =$

8. $12 \times 8 =$

9. $3 \div 3 =$

10. $4 \times 10 =$

11. $48 \div 4 =$

12. $6 \times 8 =$

13. $1 \times 5 =$

14. $4 \times 5 =$

15. $40 \div 8 =$

16. $72 \div 8 =$

17. $11 \times 10 =$

18. $22 \div 2 =$

19. $64 \div 8 =$

20. $30 \div 10 =$

Total _____ / 20 marks

Name	Class	Date

Test 28

🕐 3-4 minutes

1. $1 \times 2 =$ ☐

2. $6 \div 2 =$ ☐

3. $8 \times 7 =$ ☐

4. $30 \div 10 =$ ☐

5. $8 \times 5 =$ ☐

6. $24 \div 4 =$ ☐

7. $3 \times 5 =$ ☐

8. $10 \div 10 =$ ☐

9. $4 \times 3 =$ ☐

10. $45 \div 5 =$ ☐

11. $4 \times 9 =$ ☐

12. $10 \div 5 =$ ☐

13. $9 \times 10 =$ ☐

14. $22 \div 2 =$ ☐

15. $2 \times 8 =$ ☐

16. $20 \div 5 =$ ☐

17. $55 \div 5 =$ ☐

18. $3 \times 8 =$ ☐

19. $8 \div 4 =$ ☐

20. $80 \div 8 =$ ☐

Total _____ / 20 marks

Year 3

Name	Class	Date

Test 29

1. $3 \times 1 = \boxed{}$

2. What is twenty-eight shared between four? $\boxed{}$

3. $5 \times \boxed{} = 50$

4. Children count the legs of cows they can see in a field. If cows have 4 legs and they count 44 legs altogether, how many cows are in the field? $\boxed{}$

5. What is five multiplied by five? $\boxed{}$

6. How many groups of eight are there in seventy-two? $\boxed{}$

7. A jockey rides his horse for 11 km every day. How many kilometres would he ride in 10 days? $\boxed{}$ km

8. $70 \div \boxed{} = 7$

9. $40 \times 3 = \boxed{}$

10. A class teacher shares 24 pears equally between 8 children. How many pears do they each get? $\boxed{}$

11. $60 \times 2 =$ ☐

12. $18 \div 3 =$ ☐

13. If 2 children count all of their fingers and thumbs, how many fingers and thumbs do they have altogether? ☐

14. What is eight divided by eight? ☐

15. ☐ $\div 5 = 6$

16. There are 5 people standing in a queue. How many people's legs are there in the queue? ☐

17. $96 \div 8 =$ ☐

18. If a golfer plays 9 holes of golf and takes 5 shots to complete each hole, how many shots will the golfer take in total? ☐

19. If 12 ml of rain falls a day and there are 96 ml of water in a water butt, over how many days has the rain fallen? ☐

20. $10 \times 80 =$ ☐   **Total _____ / 20 marks**

Test 30

 5 minutes

1. $8 \times 3 =$ ☐

2. $8 \times 60 =$ ☐

3. What is ten multiplied by itself? ☐

4. $80 \div 4 =$ ☐

5. There are 8 caravans at a holiday park. If there are 4 people in each caravan, how many people are staying in caravans at the park? ☐

6. What is five multiplied by ten? ☐

7. What is twenty-one shared between three? ☐

8. $5 \times 50 =$ ☐

9. Gary plants 36 bushes in his garden. If he plants the bushes equally in 4 beds, how many bushes will he plant in each bed? ☐

10. $56 \div 8 =$ ☐

11. How many groups of three are in thirty-six? ☐

12. ☐ × 10 = 110

13. 6 × 8 = ☐

14. What is nine multiplied by three? ☐

15. A car travels 60 kilometres in an hour. If it continues at this speed, how many kilometres will the car travel in 2 hours? ☐ km

16. It takes 28 litres of paint to cover four rooms in a house. If all the rooms are of equal size, how many litres of paint does it take to paint each room? ☐ litres

17. 40 × 6 = ☐

18. 33 ÷ ☐ = 11

19. What is seven multiplied by five? ☐

20. What is ten shared between two? ☐

Total _____ / 20 marks

Year 4

6 Times Tables

7 Times Tables

9 Times Tables

11 Times Tables

12 Times Tables

Mixed 6, 7, 9, 11 and 12 Times Tables

Mixed 3, 4, 6, 7, 8, 9, 11 and 12 Times Tables

Mixed 2–12 Times Tables

Name	Class	Date

Test 1

 2 minutes

1. 1 × 6 =

2. 6 × 4 =

3. 5 × 6 =

4. 6 × 7 =

5. 2 × 6 =

6. 6 × 12 =

7. 9 × 6 =

8. 6 × 3 =

9. 8 × 6 =

10. 6 × 6 =

11. 6 × 11 =

12. 10 × 6 =

Total _____ / 12 marks

Name	Class	Date

Test 2

 2 minutes

1. 12 ÷ 6 = ☐

2. 24 ÷ 6 = ☐

3. 72 ÷ 6 = ☐

4. 36 ÷ 6 = ☐

5. 30 ÷ 6 = ☐

6. 54 ÷ 6 = ☐

7. 6 ÷ 6 = ☐

8. 66 ÷ 6 = ☐

9. 42 ÷ 6 = ☐

10. 60 ÷ 6 = ☐

11. 48 ÷ 6 = ☐

12. 18 ÷ 6 = ☐

Total _____ / 12 marks

Test 3

1. What is six shared between six? ☐

2. A farmer picks 24 kg of onions. If he stores his onions in 6 kg boxes, how many boxes will he need? ☐

3. What is six multiplied by itself? ☐

4. A man runs a kilometre every 6 minutes. At this pace, how many kilometres can he run in 30 minutes? ☐ km

5. How many groups of six make forty-eight? ☐

6. What is three multiplied by six? ☐

7. A bus route has 7 stops. If 6 people get on at each stop and nobody gets off, how many people are on the bus? ☐

8. How many groups of six make fifty-four? ☐

9. A chicken lays 12 eggs. If it lays 6 eggs a day, how many days in total has it taken to lay the eggs? ☐

10. If there are 72 children in a school and they are divided into 6 equal teams for sports day, how many children will be in each team? ☐

11. How many groups of six make sixty-six? ☐

12. Sophie is sewing some knitted squares to make a scarf. If each square is 10 cm long and she has 6 squares, how long is the scarf? ☐ cm

Total _____ / 12 marks

Test 4

 2 minutes

1. $40 \times 6 =$ ☐

2. $6 \times 700 =$ ☐

3. $20 \times 60 =$ ☐

4. $6 \times 900 =$ ☐

5. $6 \times 0.5 =$ ☐

6. $6 \times 12 =$ ☐

7. $11 \times 60 =$ ☐

8. $6 \times 3 =$ ☐

9. $100 \times 6 =$ ☐

10. $600 \times 6 =$ ☐

11. $80 \times 60 =$ ☐

12. $300 \times 6 =$ ☐

Total _____ / 12 marks

Name	Class	Date

Test 5

 2 minutes

1. 2 × 7 = ☐

2. 6 × 7 = ☐

3. 7 × 11 = ☐

4. 1 × 7 = ☐

5. 7 × 12 = ☐

6. 4 × 7 = ☐

7. 7 × 9 = ☐

8. 3 × 7 = ☐

9. 7 × 10 = ☐

10. 7 × 7 = ☐

11. 5 × 7 = ☐

12. 8 × 7 = ☐

Total _____ / 12 marks

Name	Class	Date

Test 6

 2 minutes

1. $7 \div 7 =$ ☐

2. $63 \div 7 =$ ☐

3. $49 \div 7 =$ ☐

4. $14 \div 7 =$ ☐

5. $70 \div 7 =$ ☐

6. $28 \div 7 =$ ☐

7. $84 \div 7 =$ ☐

8. $77 \div 7 =$ ☐

9. $42 \div 7 =$ ☐

10. $21 \div 7 =$ ☐

11. $35 \div 7 =$ ☐

12. $56 \div 7 =$ ☐

Total _____ / 12 marks

Year 4

Test 7

🕐 3 minutes

1. What is fourteen shared between seven? ☐

2. A boy cycles to the shop every morning for his paper round. It takes 4 minutes to get there. If he delivers papers 7 days a week, how many minutes does he travel to get to the shop each week? ☐ minutes

3. How many sevens are there in thirty-five? ☐

4. There are 42 chocolates on a plate. How many people can have 7 each? ☐

5. At school there are 7 bike racks. Each bike rack can hold 12 bikes. How many people can leave their bike in a rack at school? ☐

6. What is seven multiplied by ten? ☐

7. How many times does seven go into sixty-three? ☐

8. What is seven multiplied by one? ☐

9. A journey takes 77 minutes in total. If the news comes on the car radio 7 times during the journey, how often is the news on? ☐ minutes

10. There are 56 tadpoles in a pond and seven mother frogs. If each mother frog produced the same number of tadpoles, how many tadpoles did they each have?

☐

11. If a regular heptagon has 7 sides and each side is 7 cm in length, what is the total length of the sides of the heptagon? ☐ cm

12. What is one twenty-one shared between seven? ☐

Total _____ / 12 marks

Test 8

 2 minutes

1. 3 × 700 = ☐

2. 0.1 × 7 = ☐

3. 80 × 7 = ☐

4. 20 × 70 = ☐

5. 100 × 7 = ☐

6. 70 × 70 = ☐

7. 110 × 7 = ☐

8. 600 × 7 = ☐

9. 7 × 120 = ☐

10. 0.5 × 7 = ☐

11. 90 × 70 = ☐

12. 7 × 400 = ☐

Total _____ / 12 marks

Name	Class	Date

Test 9

 2 minutes

1. 1 × 9 =

2. 9 × 7 =

3. 3 × 9 =

4. 12 × 9 =

5. 9 × 6 =

6. 2 × 9 =

7. 9 × 11 =

8. 4 × 9 =

9. 10 × 9 =

10. 9 × 9 =

11. 8 × 9 =

12. 9 × 5 =

Total _____ / 12 marks

Year 4

Name	Class	Date

Test 10

 2 minutes

1. $9 \div 9 =$ ☐

2. $27 \div 9 =$ ☐

3. $54 \div 9 =$ ☐

4. $99 \div 9 =$ ☐

5. $36 \div 9 =$ ☐

6. $108 \div 9 =$ ☐

7. $72 \div 9 =$ ☐

8. $45 \div 9 =$ ☐

9. $63 \div 9 =$ ☐

10. $18 \div 9 =$ ☐

11. $81 \div 9 =$ ☐

12. $90 \div 9 =$ ☐

Total _____ / 12 marks

Year 4

Name	Class	Date

Test 11

1. A nonagon has 9 sides. How many sides will there be on 6 nonagons? ☐

2. What is nine multiplied by two? ☐

3. It costs £9 per person to go rock climbing. How much will it cost to take a group of 9 people? £ ☐

4. A man is 9 times older than his son. If he is 36, how old is his son? ☐

5. In a reception class children change activity 9 times in 90 minutes. How often do they change activity? ☐ minutes

6. What is twenty-seven shared between nine? ☐

7. It takes 63 minutes to jog 9 kilometres. How long does it take to jog one kilometre? ☐ minutes

8. Raffy saves £108 over 9 months. How much money does he save each month? £ ☐

9. How many nines are there in ninety-nine? ☐

10. A chef makes 9 cakes. If he cuts each cake into 8 pieces, how many pieces of cake will there be in total? ☐

11. If the laundrette washes 9 loads of laundry every hour, how many loads are washed in 5 hours? ☐

12. Morten walks 1 km a day for 9 days. How many kilometres does he walk in total? ☐ km

Total _____ / 12 marks

Name	Class	Date

Test 12

 2 minutes

1. $10 \times 9 =$ ☐

2. $9 \times 0.7 =$ ☐

3. $9 \times 90 =$ ☐

4. $0.5 \times 9 =$ ☐

5. $30 \times 90 =$ ☐

6. $11 \times 90 =$ ☐

7. $900 \times 4 =$ ☐

8. $12 \times 9 =$ ☐

9. $10 \times 9 =$ ☐

10. $9 \times 200 =$ ☐

11. $80 \times 90 =$ ☐

12. $90 \times 60 =$ ☐

Total _____ / 12 marks

Year 4

Name	Class	Date

Test 13

 2 minutes

1. 11 × 1 = ☐

2. 11 × 4 = ☐

3. 12 × 11 = ☐

4. 8 × 11 = ☐

5. 11 × 9 = ☐

6. 6 × 11 = ☐

7. 11 × 7 = ☐

8. 11 × 3 = ☐

9. 5 × 11 = ☐

10. 11 × 10 = ☐

11. 2 × 11 = ☐

12. 11 × 11 = ☐

Total _____ / 12 marks

Year 4

Test 14

 2 minutes

1. $11 \div 11 =$ ☐

2. $99 \div 11 =$ ☐

3. $55 \div 11 =$ ☐

4. $110 \div 11 =$ ☐

5. $77 \div 11 =$ ☐

6. $33 \div 11 =$ ☐

7. $44 \div 11 =$ ☐

8. $121 \div 11 =$ ☐

9. $22 \div 11 =$ ☐

10. $88 \div 11 =$ ☐

11. $132 \div 11 =$ ☐

12. $66 \div 11 =$ ☐

Total _____ / 12 marks

Test 15

 3 minutes

1. A shape with 11 sides is called a hendecagon. How many sides do 9 hendecagons have?

2. If it takes 11 minutes to walk one kilometre, how long will it take to walk three kilometres at the same speed? minutes

3. What is eleven multiplied by itself?

4. Material comes in rolls of 11 m. Marianne needs 99 m of material to make some dresses. How many rolls does she need to buy?

5. How many elevens go into eighty-eight?

6. Martha is hosting a party for her daughter's birthday. She buys 11 party bags, and each bag costs £4. How much do the bags cost in total? £

7. What is fifty-five divided by eleven?

8. A restaurant has 11 tables. If each table has 6 seats, how many people can the restaurant seat? ☐

9. What is eleven shared between eleven? ☐

10. A stamp collector has 77 stamps in a collection. He has 11 stamps from each country he has visited. How many countries has he visited? ☐

11. A fence maker has 132 m of wood in his warehouse. If he needs 11 metres of wood to make a fence panel, how many fence panels can he make with the wood? ☐

12. Rhiannon needs 110 balloons for the end of school party. If balloons come in packs of 11, how many packs does she need to buy? ☐

Total _____ **/ 12 marks**

Name	Class	Date

Test 16

 2 minutes

1. $11 \times 4 =$ ☐

2. $80 \times 11 =$ ☐

3. $50 \times 11 =$ ☐

4. $100 \times 11 =$ ☐

5. $0.1 \times 11 =$ ☐

6. $11 \times 20 =$ ☐

7. $110 \times 11 =$ ☐

8. $11 \times 30 =$ ☐

9. $120 \times 11 =$ ☐

10. $6 \times 110 =$ ☐

11. $90 \times 11 =$ ☐

12. $11 \times 70 =$ ☐

Total _____ / 12 marks

Year 4

Name	Class	Date

Test 17

 2 minutes

1. $2 \times 12 =$ ☐

2. $12 \times 4 =$ ☐

3. $7 \times 12 =$ ☐

4. $11 \times 12 =$ ☐

5. $3 \times 12 =$ ☐

6. $12 \times 9 =$ ☐

7. $12 \times 6 =$ ☐

8. $12 \times 12 =$ ☐

9. $12 \times 1 =$ ☐

10. $10 \times 12 =$ ☐

11. $8 \times 12 =$ ☐

12. $12 \times 5 =$ ☐

Total _____ / 12 marks

   Year 4

Name	Class	Date

Test 18

 2 minutes

1. 36 ÷ 12 =

2. 132 ÷ 12 =

3. 60 ÷ 12 =

4. 12 ÷ 12 =

5. 48 ÷ 12 =

6. 96 ÷ 12 =

7. 72 ÷ 12 =

8. 108 ÷ 12 =

9. 24 ÷ 12 =

10. 144 ÷ 12 =

11. 120 ÷ 12 =

12. 84 ÷ 12 =

Total _____ / 12 marks

Name	Class	Date

Test 19

 3 minutes

1. A flight to South Africa takes 12 hours. How long will it take to fly there and back? ☐ hours

2. What is eleven multiplied by twelve? ☐

3. If eggs come in packs of 12 and a baker has 108 eggs, how many packs of eggs does he have in total? ☐

4. A dodecagon has 12 sides. If each side measures 6 cm, what is the total length of the dodecagon's sides? ☐ cm

5. What is thirty-six shared between twelve? ☐

6. Archie gives £9 a month to an animal charity. How much money does he donate in 12 months? £ ☐

7. If a school has 60 pupils and they are divided equally into 12 teams for house points, how many pupils are in each team? ☐

8. If a monkey eats 8 bananas a day for 12 days, how many bananas does the monkey eat? ☐

9. What is eighty-four shared between twelve? ☐

10. A helicopter pilot works 12-hour shifts. If she works 48 hours in one week, how many shifts does she do? ☐

11. What is twelve multiplied by twelve? ☐

12. There are 120 people at a wedding and the guests sit on circular tables of 10. How many tables are there? ☐

Total _____ / 12 marks

Name	Class	Date

Test 20

1. $20 \times 12 =$ ☐

2. $0.5 \times 12 =$ ☐

3. $12 \times 100 =$ ☐

4. $30 \times 12 =$ ☐

5. $12 \times 70 =$ ☐

6. $80 \times 12 =$ ☐

7. $12 \times 9 =$ ☐

8. $120 \times 120 =$ ☐

9. $0.6 \times 12 =$ ☐

10. $11 \times 12 =$ ☐

11. $12 \times 400 =$ ☐

12. $1.2 \times 8 =$ ☐

Total _____ / 12 marks

Year 4

Test 21

1. $1 \times 6 =$ ☐

2. ☐ $\times 3 = 21$

3. $12 \times$ ☐ $= 60$

4. $11 \times 10 =$ ☐

5. ☐ $\times 6 = 18$

6. $12 \times$ ☐ $= 144$

7. $7 \times 8 =$ ☐

8. ☐ $\times 11 = 55$

9. $9 \times$ ☐ $= 72$

10. $7 \times 7 =$ ☐

11. ☐ $\times 12 = 36$

12. $9 \times$ ☐ $= 9$

13. $10 \times 6 =$ ☐

14. ☐ $\times 11 = 22$

15. $6 \times$ ☐ $= 72$

16. $12 \times 8 =$ ☐

17. ☐ $\times 7 = 63$

18. $6 \times$ ☐ $= 48$

19. $4 \times 9 =$ ☐

20. ☐ $\times 1 = 12$

21. $2 \times$ ☐ $= 24$

22. $7 \times 12 =$ ☐

23. ☐ $\times 11 = 88$

24. $5 \times$ ☐ $= 30$

25. $12 \times 9 =$ ☐

Total _____ / 25 marks

Test 22

4 minutes

1. $7 \div 7 = \boxed{}$

2. $\boxed{} \div 9 = 5$

3. $88 \div \boxed{} = 11$

4. $120 \div 10 = \boxed{}$

5. $\boxed{} \div 2 = 6$

6. $40 \div \boxed{} = 8$

7. $99 \div \boxed{} = 11$

8. $72 \div 9 = \boxed{}$

9. $\boxed{} \div 9 = 2$

10. $28 \div \boxed{} = 4$

11. $33 \div 11 = \boxed{}$

12. $\boxed{} \div 12 = 5$

13. $70 \div \boxed{} = 7$

14. $\boxed{} \div 11 = 22$

15. $42 \div \boxed{} = 6$

16. $66 \div 11 = \boxed{}$

17. $\boxed{} \div 12 = 8$

18. $8 \div \boxed{} = 1$

19. $77 \div 7 = \boxed{}$

20. $\boxed{} \div 12 = 11$

21. $48 \div \boxed{} = 6$

22. $63 \div 9 = \boxed{}$

23. $\boxed{} \div 11 = 1$

24. $90 \div \boxed{} = 9$

25. $81 \div 9 = \boxed{}$

Total _____ / 25 marks

Test 23

🕐 4 minutes

1. $400 \times 6 =$

2. $100 \times 7 =$

3. $80 \times 70 =$

4. $11 \times 100 =$

5. $70 \times 11 =$

6. $120 \times 4 =$

7. $90 \times 60 =$

8. $70 \times 80 =$

9. $11 \times 600 =$

10. $300 \times 8 =$

11. $70 \times 12 =$

12. $120 \times 6 =$

13. $90 \times 12 =$

14. $7 \times 500 =$

15. $12 \times 110 =$

16. $0.2 \times 8 =$

17. $40 \times 11 =$

18. $120 \times 9 =$

19. $600 \times 6 =$

20. $11 \times 90 =$

21. $800 \times 11 =$

22. $120 \times 2 =$

23. $90 \times 60 =$

24. $80 \times 0.7 =$

25. $0.9 \times 9 =$

Total _____ / 25 marks

Test 24

🕐 6 minutes

1. What is six multiplied by three? ☐

2. How many groups of eleven are there in fifty-five? ☐

3. Mum cooks 27 burgers at a barbecue. If there are 9 guests, how many burgers can they each have? ☐

4. A florist makes 12 bouquets for a wedding. In each bouquet there are 10 flowers. How many flowers are used? ☐

5. Trays of bedding plants are sold with 8 plants in each tray. How many plants will be in 6 trays? ☐

6. What is six times six? ☐

7. What is double six? ☐

8. A golfer takes 72 shots to complete a round of golf. If he plays 6 shots per hole, how many holes does he complete? ☐

9. What do nine groups of six equal? ☐

10. If there are 6 sheep in a pen, how many legs will the group of sheep have altogether? ☐

11. An hour is 60 minutes. How many 12-minute intervals are there in an hour? ☐

12. A class of 35 children are set in 7 equal sized groups for mathematics lessons. How many children are in each group? ☐

13. What is one multiplied by six? ☐

14. What is twelve multiplied by itself? ☐

15. How many times does twelve go into thirty-six? ☐

16. What is seventy-seven shared between eleven? ☐

17. There are 8 packs of crackers in the cupboard. If each pack contains 12 crackers, how many crackers are there in total? ☐

18. What is nine multiplied by itself? ☐

19. How many nines make seventy-two? ☐

20. What do two lots of eleven equal? ☐

21. There are seven spiders on a web. If each spider has 8 legs, how many legs will there be altogether? ☐

22. If Toby visits his grandparents once every month, how many times does he see his grandparents in one year? ☐

23. There are 90 minutes in a football match. If there is a free kick every 9 minutes, how many free kicks will there be in the game? ☐

24. What is eleven multiplied by eleven? ☐

25. There are 99 streamers needed for a party. If streamers come in packs of 9, how many packs are required? ☐

Total _____ / 25 marks

Year 4

Test 25

 6 minutes

1. $1 \times 6 =$ ☐

2. $35 \div 7 =$ ☐

3. What is eight multiplied by seven? ☐

4. There are 70 cakes in a bakery. How many people can buy 7 cakes? ☐

5. How many times does six go into thirty-six? ☐

6. ☐ $\div 11 = 12$

7. $9 \times$ ☐ $= 9$

8. What is ninety-nine shared between eleven? ☐

9. It costs £45 for 9 children to enter a theme park. How much does it cost for one child? £ ☐

10. $110 \div$ ☐ $= 10$

11. What is twelve multiplied by two? ☐

12. How many times does seven go into seventy-seven? ☐

13. If there are 42 people travelling on a train and 6 people in each carriage, how many carriages are on the train? ☐

14. What is nine multiplied by seven? ☐

15. There are 21 squares in a bar of chocolate. If there are 7 squares in a row, how many rows are in the bar? ☐

16. ☐ $\times 6 = 12$

17. A gardener plants 9 pots of marigold seeds. He puts 6 seeds in each pot. How many seeds does he plant? ☐

18. How many groups of two make eighteen? ☐

19. $60 \times 50 =$ ☐

20. $9 \times$ ☐ $= 72$

21. There are 12 eggs in a box. If it takes 6 eggs to make an omelette, how many omelettes can be made from the box of eggs? ☐

22. What is eighty-four shared between seven? ☐

23. If 60p is shared between 12 children, how many pence does each child get? ☐ p

24. $96 \div 12 =$ ☐

25. What are six groups of twelve? ☐

Total _____ **/ 25 marks**

Test 26

1. $7 \times 2 = \boxed{}$

2. $\boxed{} \times 5 = 45$

3. $11 \times \boxed{} = 55$

4. $8 \times 4 = \boxed{}$

5. $\boxed{} \times 1 = 3$

6. $12 \times \boxed{} = 72$

7. $8 \times 8 = \boxed{}$

8. $\boxed{} \times 3 = 12$

9. $8 \times \boxed{} = 80$

10. $12 \times 7 = \boxed{}$

11. $\boxed{} \times 9 = 81$

12. $7 \times \boxed{} = 28$

13. $12 \times 11 = \boxed{}$

14. $\boxed{} \times 3 = 15$

15. $4 \times \boxed{} = 44$

16. $9 \times 2 = \boxed{}$

17. $\boxed{} \times 11 = 88$

18. $12 \times \boxed{} = 24$

19. $12 \times 10 = \boxed{}$

20. $\boxed{} \times 9 = 63$

21. $1 \times \boxed{} = 11$

22. $3 \times 9 = \boxed{}$

23. $\boxed{} \times 12 = 96$

24. $11 \times \boxed{} = 99$

25. $6 \times 7 = \boxed{}$

Total _____ / 25 marks

Year 4

Test 27

🕐 4 minutes

1. $4 \div 1 = \boxed{}$

2. $\boxed{} \div 9 = 6$

3. $33 \div \boxed{} = 3$

4. $77 \div 11 = \boxed{}$

5. $\boxed{} \div 9 = 12$

6. $32 \div \boxed{} = 4$

7. $99 \div \boxed{} = 11$

8. $8 \div 8 = \boxed{}$

9. $\boxed{} \div 3 = 6$

10. $70 \div \boxed{} = 10$

11. $48 \div 12 = \boxed{}$

12. $\boxed{} \div 12 = 3$

13. $132 \div \boxed{} = 11$

14. $\boxed{} \div 9 = 9$

15. $40 \div \boxed{} = 5$

16. $16 \div 4 = \boxed{}$

17. $\boxed{} \div 12 = 1$

18. $49 \div \boxed{} = 7$

19. $66 \div 11 = \boxed{}$

20. $\boxed{} \div 11 = 9$

21. $72 \div \boxed{} = 8$

22. $21 \div 3 = \boxed{}$

23. $\boxed{} \div 8 = 11$

24. $9 \div \boxed{} = 3$

25. $22 \div 11 = \boxed{}$

Total _____ / 25 marks

Year 4

Test 28

🕐 4 minutes

1. $4 \times 100 =$ ☐

2. $0.1 \times 5 =$ ☐

3. $300 \times 9 =$ ☐

4. $12 \times 0.3 =$ ☐

5. $80 \times 600 =$ ☐

6. $40 \times 70 =$ ☐

7. $11 \times 100 =$ ☐

8. $20 \times 40 =$ ☐

9. $0.8 \times 9 =$ ☐

10. $600 \times 4 =$ ☐

11. $110 \times 7 =$ ☐

12. $300 \times 8 =$ ☐

13. $80 \times 0.1 =$ ☐

14. $800 \times 3 =$ ☐

15. $12 \times 60 =$ ☐

16. $90 \times 100 =$ ☐

17. $100 \times 30 =$ ☐

18. $0.5 \times 40 =$ ☐

19. $110 \times 11 =$ ☐

20. $700 \times 8 =$ ☐

21. $90 \times 7 =$ ☐

22. $600 \times 4 =$ ☐

23. $0.5 \times 7 =$ ☐

24. $80 \times 110 =$ ☐

25. $900 \times 7 =$ ☐

Total _____ / 25 marks

Year 4

Name	Class	Date

Test 29

1. There are 28 children playing in the park. If 4 children are playing on each piece of equipment, how many different pieces of equipment are there in the park? ☐

2. What is seven multiplied by one? ☐

3. How many groups of nine make fifty-four? ☐

4. Five children each buy three toys at the shop. How many toys do they buy altogether? ☐

5. What is two multiplied by twelve? ☐

6. A train ticket costs £9. If Mum travels with her two friends on a train journey, how much will the tickets cost altogether? £ ☐

7. How many fours are there in forty-four? ☐

8. It costs Maria £7 a day to get to work on the bus. How much does it cost her to travel to work for 5 days? £ ☐

9. What is double eleven? ☐

10. If there are 3 rabbits in a hutch, how many ears are there altogether? ☐

11. How many groups of three are there in twelve? ☐

12. What is double eight? ☐

13. What is five multiplied by six? ☐

14. A man buys 36 scones for an afternoon tea. He asks for the scones to be put into boxes of 6. How many boxes will he get? ☐

15. If 12 teams enter a cycling competition and there are 5 people in each team, how many people are competing? ☐

16. A pentagon has 5 sides. How many sides will 8 pentagons have? ☐

17. A dressmaker orders 18 m of material to make 3 dresses. How much material is needed for each dress? ☐ m

18. Aaron is measuring a nine-sided shape. Each side measures 7 cm. What is the total length of the shape's sides? ☐ cm

19. How many sevens are there in seventy-seven? ☐

20. There are 132 children at a gymnastics club. If they perform in teams of 12, how many children are in each team? ☐

21. How many times does eleven go into eighty-eight? ☐

22. What is thirty-two divided by eight? ☐

23. What do seven groups of eight equal? ☐

24. Monty is counting his one pence coins. He has 48 coins. He divides the coins into 4 equal piles. How many coins are in each pile? ☐

25. It is 49 days until Christian goes on his family holiday. How many weeks is it until he goes on holiday? ☐

Total _____ / 25 marks

Name	Class	Date

Test 30

 6 minutes

1. What is nine multiplied by two? ☐

2. 11 ÷ ☐ = 1

3. If there are 6 seats at each table in the school dinner hall, how many seats will there be at 8 tables? ☐

4. Entry for 5 people to the adventure park costs £60. How much does it cost for each person to enter? £ ☐

5. 90 × 10 = ☐

6. An athlete trains for 72 minutes. It takes her 8 minutes to run a kilometre. How many kilometres does she run? ☐ km

7. What is twelve multiplied by itself? ☐

8. ☐ ÷ 7 = 9

9. What do five groups of nine equal? ☐

10. Jared evenly deals 35 playing cards to 7 players in a card game. How many cards does each player receive? ☐

11. What is eight multiplied by two? ☐

12. $77 \div \boxed{} = 11$

13. If 6 friends each have 4 turns on 'hook the duck' at a fairground, how many turns do they have in total? $\boxed{}$

14. $0.4 \times 3 = \boxed{}$

15. What is sixty divided by six? $\boxed{}$

16. How many times does eight go into fifty-six? $\boxed{}$

17. $12 \times \boxed{} = 72$

18. $10 \times 400 = \boxed{}$

19. What is eleven multiplied by three? $\boxed{}$

20. Christina does 10 sit-ups every morning. If she does this for 11 days in a row, how many sit-ups will she do in total? $\boxed{}$

21. What is one-quarter of thirty-two? $\boxed{}$

22. Mum orders 3 pizzas for dinner. They each cost £11. How much does she need to pay for the pizzas? £ $\boxed{}$

23. What is one-third of twenty-seven? $\boxed{}$

24. $0.5 \times 20 = \boxed{}$

25. $12 \times \boxed{} = 108$ **Total _____ / 25 marks**

Name	Class	Date

Test 31

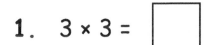 **4 minutes**

1. 3 × 3 = ☐

2. 4 × 7 = ☐

3. 11 × 6 = ☐

4. 2 × 1 = ☐

5. 6 × 6 = ☐

6. 8 × 2 = ☐

7. 12 × 9 = ☐

8. 7 × 3 = ☐

9. 5 × 9 = ☐

10. 4 × 10 = ☐

11. 12 × 4 = ☐

12. 11 × 2 = ☐

13. 8 × 7 = ☐

14. 10 × 3 = ☐

15. 2 × 6 = ☐

16. 8 × 12 = ☐

17. 1 × 11 = ☐

18. 5 × 3 = ☐

19. 11 × 9 = ☐

20. 3 × 12 = ☐

21. 7 × 9 = ☐

22. 5 × 4 = ☐

23. 11 × 6 = ☐

24. 7 × 10 = ☐

25. 8 × 5 = ☐

Total _____ / 25 marks

Test 32

🕐 4 minutes

1. $2 \times 4 = \boxed{}$

2. $\boxed{} \times 6 = 30$

3. $1 \times \boxed{} = 10$

4. $3 \times 10 = \boxed{}$

5. $\boxed{} \times 6 = 24$

6. $2 \times \boxed{} = 14$

7. $8 \times 9 = \boxed{}$

8. $\boxed{} \times 9 = 18$

9. $10 \times \boxed{} = 60$

10. $7 \times 7 = \boxed{}$

11. $\boxed{} \times 10 = 110$

12. $1 \times \boxed{} = 3$

13. $12 \times 7 = \boxed{}$

14. $\boxed{} \times 8 = 40$

15. $3 \times \boxed{} = 12$

16. $10 \times 8 = \boxed{}$

17. $\boxed{} \times 11 = 99$

18. $5 \times \boxed{} = 55$

19. $12 \times 12 = \boxed{}$

20. $\boxed{} \times 9 = 27$

21. $8 \times \boxed{} = 32$

22. $6 \times 9 = \boxed{}$

23. $\boxed{} \times 1 = 5$

24. $3 \times \boxed{} = 33$

25. $6 \times 12 = \boxed{}$

Total _____ / 25 marks

Year 4

Test 33

1. $4 \div 2 =$ ☐

2. $40 \div 10 =$ ☐

3. $42 \div 7 =$ ☐

4. $24 \div 3 =$ ☐

5. $12 \div 2 =$ ☐

6. $14 \div 7 =$ ☐

7. $108 \div 9 =$ ☐

8. $72 \div 12 =$ ☐

9. $99 \div 9 =$ ☐

10. $64 \div 8 =$ ☐

11. $45 \div 5 =$ ☐

12. $90 \div 10 =$ ☐

13. $4 \div 4 =$ ☐

14. $36 \div 6 =$ ☐

15. $77 \div 7 =$ ☐

16. $35 \div 5 =$ ☐

17. $12 \div 4 =$ ☐

18. $132 \div 11 =$ ☐

19. $20 \div 5 =$ ☐

20. $9 \div 9 =$ ☐

21. $70 \div 10 =$ ☐

22. $24 \div 8 =$ ☐

23. $22 \div 11 =$ ☐

24. $54 \div 6 =$ ☐

25. $48 \div 12 =$ ☐

Total _____ / 25 marks

Test 34

1. $3 \div 3 = \boxed{}$

2. $\boxed{} \div 2 = 9$

3. $99 \div \boxed{} = 11$

4. $49 \div 7 = \boxed{}$

5. $\boxed{} \div 8 = 9$

6. $14 \div \boxed{} = 2$

7. $40 \div 5 = \boxed{}$

8. $\boxed{} \div 6 = 5$

9. $54 \div \boxed{} = 6$

10. $80 \div 8 = \boxed{}$

11. $\boxed{} \div 12 = 12$

12. $8 \div \boxed{} = 2$

13. $55 \div 11 = \boxed{}$

14. $\boxed{} \div 7 = 12$

15. $60 \div \boxed{} = 10$

16. $12 \div 4 = \boxed{}$

17. $\boxed{} \div 9 = 3$

18. $32 \div \boxed{} = 4$

19. $110 \div 10 = \boxed{}$

20. $\boxed{} \div 4 = 6$

21. $10 \div \boxed{} = 10$

22. $24 \div 2 = \boxed{}$

23. $\boxed{} \div 11 = 4$

24. $5 \div \boxed{} = 1$

25. $81 \div 9 = \boxed{}$

Total _____ / 25 marks

Test 35

⏱ 4 minutes

1. $5 \times 4 =$

2. $20 \div 2 =$

3. $7 \times 11 =$

4. $99 \div 11 =$

5. $9 \times 6 =$

6. $49 \div 7 =$

7. $2 \times 9 =$

8. $108 \div 9 =$

9. $7 \times 10 =$

10. $48 \div 6 =$

11. $10 \times 8 =$

12. $40 \div 8 =$

13. $4 \times 11 =$

14. $84 \div 7 =$

15. $3 \times 4 =$

16. $132 \div 12 =$

17. $12 \times 12 =$

18. $10 \div 2 =$

19. $6 \times 6 =$

20. $7 \div 7 =$

21. $2 \times 11 =$

22. $15 \div 3 =$

23. $10 \times 8 =$

24. $32 \div 4 =$

25. $120 \div 10 =$

Total _____ / 25 marks

Test 36

🕐 4 minutes

1. $4 \times 3 = \boxed{}$

2. $\boxed{} \div 2 = 7$

3. $12 \times \boxed{} = 108$

4. $88 \div 8 = \boxed{}$

5. $\boxed{} \times 8 = 56$

6. $54 \div \boxed{} = 9$

7. $\boxed{} \times 7 = 35$

8. $63 \div \boxed{} = 7$

9. $12 \times 8 = \boxed{}$

10. $\boxed{} \div 11 = 12$

11. $9 \times \boxed{} = 36$

12. $48 \div 8 = \boxed{}$

13. $\boxed{} \times 12 = 84$

14. $64 \div \boxed{} = 8$

15. $4 \times 4 = \boxed{}$

16. $\boxed{} \div 9 = 5$

17. $3 \times \boxed{} = 18$

18. $120 \div 12 = \boxed{}$

19. $\boxed{} \times 8 = 72$

20. $11 \div \boxed{} = 1$

21. $2 \times 9 = \boxed{}$

22. $\boxed{} \div 6 = 6$

23. $5 \times \boxed{} = 25$

24. $100 \div 10 = \boxed{}$

25. $\boxed{} \times 9 = 81$

Total _____ / 25 marks

Year 4

Name	Class	Date

Test 37

1. $0.1 \times 3 =$ ☐

2. $40 \times 80 =$ ☐

3. $0.5 \times 9 =$ ☐

4. $20 \times 11 =$ ☐

5. $400 \times 6 =$ ☐

6. $0.7 \times 8 =$ ☐

7. $90 \times 120 =$ ☐

8. $6 \times 120 =$ ☐

9. $0.8 \times 8 =$ ☐

10. $90 \times 5 =$ ☐

11. $50 \times 5 =$ ☐

12. $90 \times 10 =$ ☐

13. $40 \times 40 =$ ☐

14. $6 \times 0.4 =$ ☐

15. $70 \times 11 =$ ☐

16. $7 \times 500 =$ ☐

17. $40 \times 12 =$ ☐

18. $1000 \times 6 =$ ☐

19. $100 \times 6 =$ ☐

20. $60 \times 50 =$ ☐

21. $30 \times 4 =$ ☐

22. $40 \times 80 =$ ☐

23. $20 \times 0.1 =$ ☐

24. $900 \times 6 =$ ☐

25. $4 \times 110 =$ ☐

Total _____ / 25 marks

Year 4

Test 38   🕐 4 minutes

1. $11 \times 80 =$ ☐

2. $60 \times 4 =$ ☐

3. $600 \times 9 =$ ☐

4. $0.7 \times 7 =$ ☐

5. $12 \times 80 =$ ☐

6. $70 \times 600 =$ ☐

7. $8 \times 800 =$ ☐

8. $6 \times 600 =$ ☐

9. $4 \times 1000 =$ ☐

10. $7 \times 1000 =$ ☐

11. $40 \times 8 =$ ☐

12. $3 \times 100 =$ ☐

13. $0.4 \times 4 =$ ☐

14. $0.1 \times 40 =$ ☐

15. $90 \times 11 =$ ☐

16. $80 \times 0.5 =$ ☐

17. $300 \times 12 =$ ☐

18. $8 \times 0.6 =$ ☐

19. $70 \times 200 =$ ☐

20. $80 \times 80 =$ ☐

21. $120 \times 6 =$ ☐

22. $9 \times 80 =$ ☐

23. $30 \times 6 =$ ☐

24. $100 \times 50 =$ ☐

25. $12 \times 90 =$ ☐

Total _____ / 25 marks

Year 4

Test 39

 6 minutes

1. What is two multiplied by itself? ☐

2. How many times does four go into sixteen? ☐

3. ☐ × 8 = 48

4. 0.9 × 10 = ☐

5. If footballs come in packs of 2, how many footballs are there in 9 packs? ☐

6. In a class of 30 children a third of the pupils have brown eyes. How many children have brown eyes? ☐

7. 12 × ☐ = 132

8. What is fifty shared between five? ☐

9. 4 × 50 = ☐

10. Dad has a £30 voucher for the garden centre and he wants to buy some plants in the £5 section. How many of these plants can he buy with his voucher? ☐

11. What is three multiplied by twelve? ☐

12. $24 \div$ ☐ $= 12$

13. $11 \times 500 =$ ☐

14. ☐ $\div 12 = 5$

15. What is eleven multiplied by ten? ☐

16. A magician pulls 49 pennies out of a hat. If he shares the pennies equally between 7 children, how many pennies does each child get? ☐

17. $12 \times 9 =$ ☐

18. What is sixty-three divided into nine equal groups? ☐

19. It takes a racing car driver 2 minutes to complete a full lap of the track. How long would it take to complete 9 laps of the track? ☐ minutes

20. There are 18 lollipops and 6 children. If they are shared equally, how many lollipops can each child have? ☐

21. $5 \times 9 =$ ☐

22. The length of the school pool is 12 m. If Veejay swims 6 lengths, how many metres does he swim altogether?

 m

23. 40 ÷ ⬚ = 5

24. What do ten groups of seven equal? ⬚

25. What is eight multiplied by three? ⬚

Total _____ **/ 25 marks**

Name	Class	Date

Test 40

 6 minutes

1. 30 × 30 = ▢

2. 8 ÷ 4 = ▢

3. Jenna looks after 10 horses. If they each eat 7 kg of horse feed per week, how much horse feed does she need each week? ▢ kg

4. If Lennon cycles for 15 minutes and it takes him 5 minutes to travel 1 kilometre, how far does he cycle? ▢ km

5. 10 × ▢ = 10

6. What is fifty-four shared between nine? ▢

7. What is double eight? ▢

8. Gianni has a party and invites 18 children. A third of the children are girls. How many girls are invited to the party? ▢

9. 12 × ▢ = 84

10. What is a quarter of 120? ▢

11. 0.8 × 8 = ▢

12. What is a tenth of ninety? ▢

       Year 4

13. How many kilometres will a car travel in 4 hours if it is travelling at a speed of 60 km per hour? ☐ km

14. What is eleven multiplied by itself? ☐

15. $6 \times 7 =$ ☐

16. If a mother is 40 years old and she is 5 times older than her daughter, how old is her daughter? ☐ years

17. On an allotment patch there are 5 rows of carrots growing. In each row there are 20 carrots. How many carrots are there altogether? ☐

18. $640 \div 8 =$ ☐

19. What do five groups of twelve equal? ☐

20. How many eights are there in seventy-two? ☐

21. $0.2 \times 5 =$ ☐

22. If there are 28 days in February and 7 days in a week, how many weeks are there in February? ☐

23. $121 \div$ ☐ $= 11$

24. What is one-third of thirty? ☐

25. If a hexagon has 6 sides, how many sides are there on 8 hexagons?

☐

Total _____ / 25 marks

Year 2 Times Tables Answers

Test 1

1	2
2	16
3	14
4	4
5	8
6	12
7	6
8	18
9	10
10	20

Test 2

1	6
2	22
3	10
4	12
5	18
6	24
7	20
8	8
9	14
10	16

Test 3

1	1
2	2
3	9
4	5
5	4
6	6
7	8
8	3
9	7
10	11

Test 4

1	2
2	9
3	10
4	3
5	6
6	5
7	7
8	8
9	4
10	11

Test 5

1	6
2	5
3	10
4	7
5	22
6	18
7	20
8	3
9	1
10	6

Test 6

1	20
2	14
3	6
4	16
5	24
6	22
7	12
8	10
9	18
10	8

Test 7

1	22
2	9
3	7
4	20
5	6
6	2
7	4
8	3
9	10
10	2

Test 8

1	40
2	35
3	55
4	15
5	45
6	25
7	20
8	50
9	30
10	60

Test 9

1	15
2	45
3	60
4	30
5	55
6	20
7	40
8	10
9	35
10	25

Year 2 Times Tables Answers

Test 10

1	2
2	4
3	9
4	11
5	3
6	12
7	10
8	6
9	5
10	7

Test 11

1	11
2	7
3	3
4	9
5	2
6	8
7	1
8	10
9	6
10	5

Test 12

1	25
2	50
3	3
4	8
5	20
6	35
7	9
8	6
9	12
10	55

Test 13

1	1
2	9
3	15
4	50
5	60
6	6
7	7
8	4
9	10
10	55

Test 14

1	8
2	6
3	20
4	35
5	25
6	3
7	4
8	45
9	10
10	12

Test 15

1	10
2	80
3	20
4	100
5	70
6	50
7	30
8	110
9	60
10	90

Test 16

1	90
2	10
3	20
4	50
5	110
6	120
7	100
8	30
9	40
10	60

Test 17

1	8
2	12
3	2
4	6
5	4
6	10
7	3
8	7
9	5
10	9

Test 18

1	2
2	4
3	6
4	9
5	11
6	5
7	10
8	3
9	12
10	7

Year 2 Times Tables Answers

Test 19

1	40
2	5
3	90
4	7
5	3
6	100
7	1
8	12
9	20
10	110

Test 20

1	80
2	7
3	120
4	5
5	60
6	9
7	20
8	3
9	100
10	4

Test 21

1	4
2	2
3	10
4	9
5	70
6	8
7	120
8	110
9	3
10	50

Test 22

1	20
2	35
3	20
4	60
5	4
6	50
7	12
8	45
9	6
10	100
11	80
12	22
13	15
14	55
15	24

Test 23

1	10
2	40
3	40
4	8
5	70
6	60
7	18
8	16
9	120
10	90
11	14
12	30
13	110
14	30
15	25

Test 24

1	5
2	7
3	3
4	2
5	7
6	10
7	8
8	12
9	5
10	10
11	4
12	7
13	8
14	12
15	12

Year 2 Times Tables Answers

Test 25

1	1
2	10
3	5
4	8
5	9
6	6
7	11
8	3
9	1
10	6
11	12
12	4
13	2
14	9
15	6

Test 26

1	1
2	10
3	10
4	8
5	12
6	6
7	10
8	20
9	11
10	22
11	9
12	9
13	3
14	11
15	3

Test 27

1	10
2	4
3	100
4	80
5	6
6	7
7	70
8	8
9	18
10	8
11	10
12	30
13	10
14	45
15	8

Test 28

1	15
2	6
3	3
4	5
5	5
6	14
7	70
8	7
9	40
10	5
11	40
12	30
13	8
14	20
15	12

Test 29

1	100
2	40
3	300
4	80
5	160
6	60
7	70
8	120
9	50
10	120
11	60
12	40
13	200
14	100
15	140

Test 30

1	55
2	10
3	80
4	50
5	10
6	14
7	6
8	25
9	20
10	60
11	12
12	16
13	4
14	12
15	110

Year 3 Times Tables Answers

Test 1

1	6
2	18
3	36
4	9
5	24
6	12
7	21
8	15
9	30
10	27
11	3
12	33

Test 2

1	2
2	3
3	24
4	12
5	3
6	3
7	12
8	6
9	27
10	21
11	11
12	1

Test 3

1	36
2	10
3	3
4	12
5	12
6	11
7	27
8	24
9	15
10	7
11	30
12	6

Test 4

1	300
2	60
3	180
4	270
5	60
6	210
7	36
8	240
9	120
10	330
11	150
12	90

Test 5

1	15
2	33
3	7
4	12
5	24
6	12
7	6
8	9
9	9
10	10
11	8
12	60

Test 6

1	4
2	28
3	8
4	40
5	20
6	48
7	44
8	16
9	24
10	32
11	12
12	36

Year 3 Times Tables Answers

Test 7

1	1
2	11
3	4
4	9
5	4
6	4
7	48
8	2
9	4
10	24
11	10
12	8

Test 8

1	20
2	44
3	1
4	32
5	2
6	3
7	6
8	12
9	36
10	4
11	28
12	10

Test 9

1	400
2	44
3	200
4	48
5	280
6	160
7	320
8	360
9	120
10	240
11	400
12	80

Test 10

1	8
2	7
3	10
4	4
5	16
6	48
7	4
8	11
9	9
10	20
11	3
12	6

Test 11

1	16
2	8
3	72
4	80
5	96
6	24
7	40
8	32
9	48
10	88
11	56
12	64

Test 12

1	56
2	10
3	3
4	4
5	3
6	8
7	48
8	5
9	2
10	72
11	12
12	11

Year 3 Times Tables Answers

Test 13

1	40
2	48
3	9
4	16
5	96
6	10
7	64
8	5
9	56
10	4
11	3
12	88

Test 14

1	80
2	240
3	400
4	720
5	800
6	88
7	480
8	560
9	96
10	640
11	160
12	320

Test 15

1	48
2	5
3	96
4	64
5	80
6	6
7	7
8	3
9	9
10	88
11	16
12	8

Test 16

1	3
2	18
3	24
4	80
5	8
6	30
7	96
8	28
9	48
10	44
11	12
12	16
13	56
14	20
15	9
16	32
17	36
18	4
19	64
20	36

Test 17

1	8
2	21
3	16
4	24
5	40
6	27
7	28
8	33
9	72
10	3
11	88
12	8
13	15
14	64
15	18
16	48
17	56
18	24
19	18
20	44

Test 18

1	6
2	4
3	4
4	28
5	6
6	9
7	24
8	8
9	8
10	56
11	2
12	5
13	96
14	6
15	4
16	36
17	8
18	8
19	44
20	12

Year 3 Times Tables Answers

Test 19

1	2
2	3
3	3
4	9
5	4
6	11
7	12
8	7
9	6
10	8
11	7
12	3
13	6
14	9
15	11
16	2
17	10
18	5
19	9
20	5

Test 20

1	3
2	10
3	9
4	10
5	8
6	7
7	12
8	8
9	56
10	16
11	36
12	5
13	3
14	1
15	64
16	6
17	96
18	11
19	36
20	8

Test 21

1	30
2	3
3	72
4	15
5	7
6	27
7	11
8	2
9	32
10	6
11	8
12	12
13	10
14	48
15	24
16	11
17	56
18	5
19	16
20	36

Year 3 Times Tables Answers

Test 22

1	8
2	8
3	21
4	16
5	10
6	9
7	7
8	11
9	72
10	3
11	11
12	8
13	18
14	5
15	8
16	8
17	56
18	48
19	6
20	44

Test 23

1	16
2	36
3	60
4	40
5	120
6	30
7	14
8	36
9	33
10	24
11	80
12	12
13	20
14	88
15	48
16	56
17	24
18	40
19	21
20	6

Test 24

1	3
2	32
3	8
4	25
5	28
6	22
7	30
8	70
9	18
10	90
11	24
12	9
13	110
14	96
15	4
16	40
17	10
18	72
19	60
20	18

Year 3 Times Tables Answers

Test 25

1	2
2	5
3	6
4	8
5	11
6	11
7	4
8	5
9	6
10	6
11	6
12	2
13	9
14	8
15	9
16	8
17	10
18	7
19	12
20	9

Test 26

1	3
2	4
3	7
4	11
5	9
6	8
7	12
8	12
9	7
10	6
11	10
12	3
13	7
14	7
15	6
16	9
17	11
18	9
19	12
20	11

Test 27

1	10
2	10
3	56
4	5
5	9
6	100
7	2
8	96
9	1
10	40
11	12
12	48
13	5
14	20
15	5
16	9
17	110
18	11
19	8
20	3

Year 3 Times Tables Answers

Test 28

1	2
2	3
3	56
4	3
5	40
6	6
7	15
8	1
9	12
10	9
11	36
12	2
13	90
14	11
15	16
16	4
17	11
18	24
19	2
20	10

Test 29

1	3
2	7
3	10
4	11
5	25
6	9
7	110
8	10
9	120
10	3
11	120
12	6
13	20
14	1
15	30
16	10
17	12
18	45
19	8
20	800

Test 30

1	24
2	480
3	100
4	20
5	32
6	50
7	7
8	250
9	9
10	7
11	12
12	11
13	48
14	27
15	120
16	7
17	240
18	3
19	35
20	5

Year 4 Times Tables Answers

Test 1

1	6
2	24
3	30
4	42
5	12
6	72
7	54
8	18
9	48
10	36
11	66
12	60

Test 2

1	2
2	4
3	12
4	6
5	5
6	9
7	1
8	11
9	7
10	10
11	8
12	3

Test 3

1	1
2	4
3	36
4	5
5	8
6	18
7	42
8	9
9	2
10	12
11	11
12	60

Test 4

1	240
2	4200
3	1200
4	5400
5	3
6	72
7	660
8	18
9	600
10	3600
11	4800
12	1800

Test 5

1	14
2	42
3	77
4	7
5	84
6	28
7	63
8	21
9	70
10	49
11	35
12	56

Test 6

1	1
2	9
3	7
4	2
5	10
6	4
7	12
8	11
9	6
10	3
11	5
12	8

Year 4 Times Tables Answers

Test 7

1	2
2	28
3	5
4	6
5	84
6	70
7	9
8	7
9	11
10	8
11	49
12	3

Test 8

1	2100
2	0.7
3	560
4	1400
5	700
6	4900
7	770
8	4200
9	840
10	3.5
11	6300
12	2800

Test 9

1	9
2	63
3	27
4	108
5	54
6	18
7	99
8	36
9	90
10	81
11	72
12	45

Test 10

1	1
2	3
3	6
4	11
5	4
6	12
7	8
8	5
9	7
10	2
11	9
12	10

Test 11

1	54
2	18
3	81
4	4
5	10
6	3
7	7
8	12
9	11
10	72
11	45
12	9

Test 12

1	90
2	6.3
3	810
4	4.5
5	2700
6	990
7	3600
8	108
9	90
10	1800
11	7200
12	5400

Year 4 Times Tables Answers

Test 13

1	11
2	44
3	132
4	88
5	99
6	66
7	77
8	33
9	55
10	110
11	22
12	121

Test 14

1	1
2	9
3	5
4	10
5	7
6	3
7	4
8	11
9	2
10	8
11	12
12	6

Test 15

1	99
2	33
3	121
4	9
5	8
6	44
7	5
8	66
9	1
10	7
11	12
12	10

Test 16

1	44
2	880
3	550
4	1100
5	1.1
6	220
7	1210
8	330
9	1320
10	660
11	990
12	770

Test 17

1	24
2	48
3	84
4	132
5	36
6	108
7	72
8	144
9	12
10	120
11	96
12	60

Test 18

1	3
2	11
3	5
4	1
5	4
6	8
7	6
8	9
9	2
10	12
11	10
12	7

Year 4 Times Tables Answers

Test 19

1	24
2	132
3	9
4	72
5	3
6	108
7	5
8	96
9	7
10	4
11	144
12	12

Test 20

1	240
2	6
3	1200
4	360
5	840
6	960
7	108
8	14 400
9	7.2
10	132
11	4800
12	9.6

Test 21

1	6
2	7
3	5
4	110
5	3
6	12
7	56
8	5
9	8
10	49
11	3
12	1
13	60
14	2
15	12
16	96
17	9
18	8
19	36
20	12
21	12
22	84
23	8
24	6
25	108

Year 4 Times Tables Answers

Test 22

1	1
2	45
3	8
4	12
5	12
6	5
7	9
8	8
9	18
10	7
11	3
12	60
13	10
14	2
15	7
16	6
17	96
18	8
19	11
20	132
21	8
22	7
23	11
24	10
25	9

Test 23

1	2400
2	700
3	5600
4	1100
5	770
6	480
7	5400
8	5600
9	6600
10	2400
11	840
12	720
13	1080
14	3500
15	1320
16	1.6
17	440
18	1080
19	3600
20	990
21	8800
22	240
23	5400
24	56
25	8.1

Test 24

1	18
2	5
3	3
4	120
5	48
6	36
7	12
8	12
9	54
10	24
11	5
12	5
13	6
14	144
15	3
16	7
17	96
18	81
19	8
20	22
21	56
22	12
23	10
24	121
25	11

Year 4 Times Tables Answers

Test 25

1	6
2	5
3	56
4	10
5	6
6	132
7	1
8	9
9	5
10	11
11	24
12	11
13	7
14	63
15	3
16	2
17	54
18	9
19	3000
20	8
21	2
22	12
23	5
24	8
25	72

Test 26

1	14
2	9
3	5
4	32
5	3
6	6
7	64
8	4
9	10
10	84
11	9
12	4
13	132
14	5
15	11
16	18
17	8
18	2
19	120
20	7
21	11
22	27
23	8
24	9
25	42

Test 27

1	4
2	54
3	11
4	7
5	108
6	8
7	9
8	1
9	18
10	7
11	4
12	36
13	12
14	81
15	8
16	4
17	12
18	7
19	6
20	99
21	9
22	7
23	88
24	3
25	2

Year 4 Times Tables Answers

Test 28

1	400
2	0.5
3	2700
4	3.6
5	48 000
6	2800
7	1100
8	800
9	7.2
10	2400
11	770
12	2400
13	8
14	2400
15	720
16	9000
17	3000
18	20
19	1210
20	5600
21	630
22	2400
23	3.5
24	8800
25	6300

Test 29

1	7
2	7
3	6
4	15
5	24
6	27
7	11
8	35
9	22
10	6
11	4
12	16
13	30
14	6
15	60
16	40
17	6
18	63
19	11
20	11
21	8
22	4
23	56
24	12
25	7

Test 30

1	18
2	11
3	48
4	12
5	900
6	9
7	144
8	63
9	45
10	5
11	16
12	7
13	24
14	1.2
15	10
16	7
17	6
18	4000
19	33
20	110
21	8
22	33
23	9
24	10
25	9

Year 4 Times Tables Answers

Test 31

1	9
2	28
3	66
4	2
5	36
6	16
7	108
8	21
9	45
10	40
11	48
12	22
13	56
14	30
15	12
16	96
17	11
18	15
19	99
20	36
21	63
22	20
23	66
24	70
25	40

Test 32

1	8
2	5
3	10
4	30
5	4
6	7
7	72
8	2
9	6
10	49
11	11
12	3
13	84
14	5
15	4
16	80
17	9
18	11
19	144
20	3
21	4
22	54
23	5
24	11
25	72

Test 33

1	2
2	4
3	6
4	8
5	6
6	2
7	12
8	6
9	11
10	8
11	9
12	9
13	1
14	6
15	11
16	7
17	3
18	12
19	4
20	1
21	7
22	3
23	2
24	9
25	4

Year 4 Times Tables Answers

Test 34

1	1
2	18
3	9
4	7
5	72
6	7
7	8
8	30
9	9
10	10
11	144
12	4
13	5
14	84
15	6
16	3
17	27
18	8
19	11
20	24
21	1
22	12
23	44
24	5
25	9

Test 35

1	20
2	10
3	77
4	9
5	54
6	7
7	18
8	12
9	70
10	8
11	80
12	5
13	44
14	12
15	12
16	11
17	144
18	5
19	36
20	1
21	22
22	5
23	80
24	8
25	12

Test 36

1	12
2	14
3	9
4	11
5	7
6	6
7	5
8	9
9	96
10	132
11	4
12	6
13	7
14	8
15	16
16	45
17	6
18	10
19	9
20	11
21	18
22	36
23	5
24	10
25	9

Year 4 Times Tables Answers

Test 37

1	0.3
2	3200
3	4.5
4	220
5	2400
6	5.6
7	10 800
8	720
9	6.4
10	450
11	250
12	900
13	1600
14	2.4
15	770
16	3500
17	480
18	6000
19	600
20	3000
21	120
22	3200
23	2
24	5400
25	440

Test 38

1	880
2	240
3	5400
4	4.9
5	960
6	42 000
7	6400
8	3600
9	4000
10	7000
11	320
12	300
13	1.6
14	4
15	990
16	40
17	3600
18	4.8
19	14 000
20	6400
21	720
22	720
23	180
24	5000
25	1080

Test 39

1	4
2	4
3	6
4	9
5	18
6	10
7	11
8	10
9	200
10	6
11	36
12	2
13	5500
14	60
15	110
16	7
17	108
18	7
19	18
20	3
21	45
22	72
23	8
24	70
25	24

Year 4 Times Tables Answers

Test 40

1	900
2	2
3	70
4	3
5	1
6	6
7	16
8	6
9	7
10	30
11	6.4
12	9
13	240
14	121
15	42
16	8
17	100
18	80
19	60
20	9
21	1
22	4
23	11
24	10
25	48

Name _____   Class _____

Year 2 Times Tables Record Sheet

Test	Description	Mark	Total marks	👏	👍	✋
1	2x table		10			
2	2x table		10			
3	2x table		10			
4	2x table		10			
5	2x table		10			
6	2x table		10			
7	2x table		10			
8	5x table		10			
9	5x table		10			
10	5x table		10			
11	5x table		10			
12	5x table		10			
13	5x table		10			
14	5x table		10			
15	10x table		10			
16	10x table		10			
17	10x table		10			
18	10x table		10			
19	10x table		10			
20	10x table		10			
21	10x table		10			
22	Mixed 2x, 5x, 10x tables		15			
23	Mixed 2x, 5x, 10x tables		15			
24	Mixed 2x, 5x, 10x tables		15			
25	Mixed 2x, 5x, 10x tables		15			
26	Mixed 2x, 5x, 10x tables		15			
27	Mixed 2x, 5x, 10x tables		15			
28	Mixed 2x, 5x, 10x tables		15			
29	Mixed 2x, 5x, 10x tables		15			
30	Mixed 2x, 5x, 10x tables		15			

I really enjoyed it.

I did well.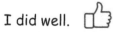

A bit challenging and I need more practice.

Name _____ Class _____

Year 3 Times Tables Record Sheet

Test	Description	Mark	Total marks	👏	👍	✋
1	3x table		12			
2	3x table		12			
3	3x table		12			
4	3x table		12			
5	3x table		12			
6	4x table		12			
7	4x table		12			
8	4x table		12			
9	4x table		12			
10	4x table		12			
11	8x table		12			
12	8x table		12			
13	8x table		12			
14	8x table		12			
15	8x table		12			
16	Mixed 3x, 4x, 8x tables		20			
17	Mixed 3x, 4x, 8x tables		20			
18	Mixed 3x, 4x, 8x tables		20			
19	Mixed 3x, 4x, 8x tables		20			
20	Mixed 3x, 4x, 8x tables		20			
21	Mixed 3x, 4x, 8x tables		20			
22	Mixed 3x, 4x, 8x tables		20			
23	Mixed 2x, 3x, 4x, 5x, 8x, 10x tables		20			
24	Mixed 2x, 3x, 4x, 5x, 8x, 10x tables		20			
25	Mixed 2x, 3x, 4x, 5x, 8x, 10x tables		20			
26	Mixed 2x, 3x, 4x, 5x, 8x, 10x tables		20			
27	Mixed 2x, 3x, 4x, 5x, 8x, 10x tables		20			
28	Mixed 2x, 3x, 4x, 5x, 8x, 10x tables		20			
29	Mixed 2x, 3x, 4x, 5x, 8x, 10x tables		20			
30	Mixed 2x, 3x, 4x, 5x, 8x, 10x tables		20			

I really enjoyed it. 👏

I did well. 👍

A bit challenging and I need more practice. ✋

Name _____   Class _____

Year 4 Times Tables Record Sheet

Test	Description	Mark	Total marks		👍	✋
1	6x table		12			
2	6x table		12			
3	6x table		12			
4	6x table		12			
5	7x table		12			
6	7x table		12			
7	7x table		12			
8	7x table		12			
9	9x table		12			
10	9x table		12			
11	9x table		12			
12	9x table		12			
13	11x table		12			
14	11x table		12			
15	11x table		12			
16	11x table		12			
17	12x table		12			
18	12x table		12			
19	12x table		12			
20	12x table		12			
21	Mixed 6x, 7x, 9x, 11x, 12x tables		25			
22	Mixed 6x, 7x, 9x, 11x, 12x tables		25			
23	Mixed 6x, 7x, 9x, 11x, 12x tables		25			
24	Mixed 6x, 7x, 9x, 11x, 12x tables		25			
25	Mixed 6x, 7x, 9x, 11x, 12x tables		25			
26	Mixed 3x, 4x, 6x, 7x, 8x, 9x, 11x, 12x tables		25			
27	Mixed 3x, 4x, 6x, 7x, 8x, 9x, 11x, 12x tables		25			
28	Mixed 3x, 4x, 6x, 7x, 8x, 9x, 11x, 12x tables		25			
29	Mixed 3x, 4x, 6x, 7x, 8x, 9x, 11x, 12x tables		25			
30	Mixed 3x, 4x, 6x, 7x, 8x, 9x, 11x, 12x tables		25			

I really enjoyed it.

I did well.

A bit challenging and I need more practice.

Name _____   Class _____

Year 4 Times Tables Record Sheet

Test	Description	Mark	Total marks	👏	👍	✋
31	Mixed 2-12x tables		25			
32	Mixed 2-12x tables		25			
33	Mixed 2-12x tables		25			
34	Mixed 2-12x tables		25			
35	Mixed 2-12x tables		25			
36	Mixed 2-12x tables		25			
37	Mixed 2-12x tables		25			
38	Mixed 2-12x tables		25			
39	Mixed 2-12x tables		25			
40	Mixed 2-12x tables		25			

I really enjoyed it.

I did well. 👍

A bit challenging and I need more practice. ✋